ONTARIO FIRESIDE GHOST STORIES

ONTARIO FIRESIDE GHOST STORIES

Barbara Smith

GHOST
HOUSE

Ghost House Books

The Distributor: Lone Pine Publishing
10145 – 81 Avenue
Edmonton, AB T6E 1W9
Canada

Websites: www.ghostbooks.net
         www.lonepinepublishing.com

Library and Archives Canada Cataloguing in Publication

Smith, Barbara, 1947-
     Ontario fireside ghost stories / Barbara Smith.

ISBN 978-1-55105-875-7

     1. Ghosts--Ontario. 2. Legends--Ontario. I. Title.

GR580.S595 2011   398.209713'05   C2011-901357-6

Editorial Director: Nancy Foulds
Project Editor: Sheila Quinlan, Wendy Pirk
Production Manager: Gene Longson
Layout and Production: Lisa Morley
Cover Design: Gerry Dotto
Cover Images: Forest Background - © 2011 Thinkstock, Face In Fire -
© Thinkstock LLC, Fire - © Photos.com

We acknowledge the financial support of the Government of Canada
through the Book Publishing Industry Development Program (BPIDP) for
our publishing activities.

 Canadian   Patrimoine
Heritage   canadien

Dedication

For Amy, Andrew and David
(and their terrific parents of course too).

Acknowledgements

Thanks as always to everyone at Lone Pine Publishing, especially Shane Kennedy, Nancy Foulds, Sheila Quinlan, Wendy Pirk, Gene Longson, Gerry Dotto, Lisa Morley, Ken Davis and Tom Lore. The support and enthusiasm you've put toward my work over the years have meant the world to me. Special thanks as always to Bob for your endless patience and skillful proofreading.

Disclaimer

Although the stories in this book are set in specific Ontario locations, the characters and events described are works of fiction, strictly figments of my imagination. That's my story and I'm sticking to it.

Contents

Chapter 3: Full Moon

Twin Terror

Playing with Time

The Haunted Ghost Walk

Roses Aren't Difficult Here

A Certain Look

The Same Silly Spooky Story

Saving Grace

I Can Take You…

The First Cottage

The Figurines

What a Celebration

The Last Vampire

Hidden Treasure

The Death of You

Chapter 4: Last Quarter

A Morning Walk

Her Picture

A Daughter's Devotion

Fate

Past Death Do Us Part

Love Paid the Debt

The Pilot's Life

Tales from the Canadian Crypt

A Deal to Die For

The Dead and Breakfast

The Jacket

The Last Season

Things in the Closet

Chapter 1: New Moon

The Ride

When Anthony Knight came upon the cemetery, he wasn't sure how long he had been walking. It seemed like forever, but he knew it was probably only an hour or so. His car—what was left of it, anyway—was no more than a couple of kilometres back. But with no moon to guide him and a couple of broken ribs making him wince with every step, the progress had been slow and painful. The rain made it worse. It was the kind of downpour that folks called a "soaker"—good for the gardens but bad for somebody who was hurt and trying to find help. It was coming down not in drops but in sheets, drenching Anthony's light clothing and plastering his hair to his throbbing skull. It had turned the rutted dirt road on the outskirts of town into slippery muck that was persistently working its way into Anthony's shoes. With every step he felt worms of mud squish up between his toes. He was shivering from the cold and wet, miserable with pain and desperate to get to a telephone. And now, on top of all that, he had to pass a cemetery.

Anthony hated cemeteries—even the nice ones that were made to look like parks, with benches and shrubberies and artistic bits of statuary. It didn't matter how tidy a graveyard was, there was no hiding the truth of what lay beneath: rows and rows of corpses in various grim stages of decay, from putrefying meat to brittle bones. Since boyhood, he had lived with an unshakeable fear that the dead could reach out and grasp him with their skeletal fingers and pull him down into the cold and dark. He'd only ever confessed that fear to one person, his mother. Mrs. Knight didn't understand and wasn't able to comfort her son. She had shown only vague irritation with his foolishness. "Everybody dies, Anthony," she told him. "We'll all be in the family plot someday."

Not me, Anthony had silently vowed. *Not me.*

He had seen the family plot, with the elaborately carved armoured knight symbolizing his surname atop a central granite monument. The idea of taking a permanent nap in its cool shadow was unthinkable. Anthony accepted the inevitability of death, but not of burial. There were other options. He didn't have to end up in a cemetery.

He did occasionally have to walk past one, though. Anthony looked up and down the dark road, hoping a detour might appear out of the gloom, but none did. There was only the one narrow lane, drowning in shadows, running close by the cemetery's wrought-iron fence with its gothic spires and leaning front gates. Anthony wiped the rainwater from his eyes and took a deep breath, flinching with pain as his lungs pushed against his rib cage. There was really no decision to make; he knew that. He needed to get to the next town. He needed to see a doctor, have his ribs taped up. And he needed to call his wife so she wouldn't worry. That's what he needed to do.

But first he needed to get by this graveyard. "Just do it. Just walk," he told himself. And eventually, he did. He put one muddy foot in front of the other and began to make his slow way past the cemetery. He kept his eyes trained straight ahead, ignoring the overgrown tombstones and sculptures that loomed palely in the darkness. The wind picked up a little and a rusted hinge on the gate groaned, but Anthony just kept walking. He could do it. He *would* do it. Everything was okay, no problem.

And there was no problem—until a sudden, blinding flash of white lit the air surrounding him. Anthony was suddenly face-to-face with a wraith, its features bleached white and staring blankly, its arms outstretched to him like the grasping dead of his nightmares.

"Holy Mother!" he shrieked, but his words were swallowed by the spectre's guttural roar. It was a low rumble that grew louder each second. There was something familiar in the sound, and something confusing. The ghost floated in front of Anthony, but its growling cry came from behind…

It was a motor. In one single gratitude-filled moment, Anthony understood that there was a car coming up the road behind him and that the terrifying pale image had been headlights reflecting off a towering, particularly gruesome-looking stone angel. He felt weak with relief. He wanted to sink to his knees and weep, but he couldn't waste that kind of time or energy. Instead, he turned to face the vehicle and moved to stand directly in the blinding wash of its headlights. Painfully, he raised his arms above his head and waved them back and forth. He thought this gesture was better than sticking out his thumb. He wanted to be clear that he was no common hitchhiker.

The car slowed as it approached. Anthony held out one hand to block some of the glare and squinted in the direction of the darkened windshield, trying to see the driver. As his eyes began to adjust, the car came to a full stop. Anthony stepped over to the passenger side door, crouched as much as his pained ribs would allow, and looked into the vehicle. There was a mechanical buzz as the window magically rolled halfway down to reveal a white-faced young man with ink-black hair and a worried expression peering out at him.

"Thank you for stopping," Anthony said.

The kid nodded, but his brow was knit in a way that indicated he hadn't quite decided whether to stay stopped or not. "Car trouble?" he asked as he looked Anthony over.

Anthony wiped his dripping hair away from his face and nodded. "Yeah, you could say that," he said. "It's back thataway, halfway down a hill and wrapped around a tree. It's been a helluva night. If you could just give me a ride into Dickinson's Landing…" Anthony trailed off, too exhausted to explain further. He stood, shoulders sagging, rain pooling in his ears and running off the tip of his nose, as the stranger sized him up and made a decision.

"You look too messed up to be dangerous," the kid finally said. "Get in. Seriously. Grab that blanket out of the back to wrap up in."

Anthony reached behind the passenger seat and pulled out an itchy bundle of tartan. He wrapped it around himself, grateful for the warmth, though he was fully aware that the driver was more concerned about his upholstery than Anthony's comfort. As he settled into the low-slung passenger seat, he could see why. The car had to be some kind of custom job. Anthony had never been in a vehicle with such sleek lines and strange gadgets. European, he supposed. Even the pulsing music on the radio was oddly foreign. Anthony had never heard the like.

"So you went off the road, huh?" said the kid as he put the car back in gear and began to drive. "Your ride must be way down the ravine; I didn't see a thing back there." He cast a sideways glance at Anthony and shook his head. "You look busted up, man."

Anthony watched out the window and let his breath out in a silent whoosh once they had cleared the cemetery. "Sorry—what?" he said, suddenly aware of the silent space that meant it was his turn to talk.

"Are you, like, hurt bad?" the kid asked.

Anthony nodded. The simple motion made a bright pain flare behind his eyes. His head began to throb in sync with the strange music. "Yeah, I think I hit my head. Maybe cracked a couple ribs."

The kid shook his head in sympathy. "You're lucky I came along," he said. "My family's got a cabin by the river, back there. That's the only reason I'm on this dirt trail. And I've never seen anyone else out here. I didn't think people used it anymore. Where were you headed, anyway? Did you get lost or something? Take a wrong turn?"

"No, I wasn't lost," Anthony said. "I was heading up to…"

The kid waited patiently for Anthony to finish the sentence. But he couldn't. He brought his hands up to his face and massaged his temples with his fingers, but it didn't help. He couldn't remember where he had been going. And there was something in the way the kid was looking at him, something about the sheen of his pale face in the eerie reflection of dashboard lights that made

Anthony feel blank and lost. He shook himself, tried to lose the feeling. "Sorry," he said. "Bump on the head, you know? My memory isn't working the way it ought to."

"Don't sweat it," the kid said. He spoke lightly, but there was something in his voice that made Anthony shiver.

The cemetery, Anthony thought. *I met him right beside the cemetery.* But it was a ridiculous thought, and he scolded himself immediately for his foolishness. When he emerged from his paranoid thoughts, the kid was talking again.

"You said Dickinson's Landing?" he asked.

"Yes!" Anthony nodded with relief. "That's where I was going. Where I *am* going."

The kid shook his head. "But it's gone, man. You know that, right? Dickinson's Landing was one of the towns they flooded, one of the Lost Villages."

Anthony was confused. "I don't know anything about who flooded what, but Dickinson's Landing is just ahead. There's a service station right by the tracks, after you turn off the highway. And a diner that stays open late—it's got pay phones. There's even a doctor who lives nearby."

The kid was looking at Anthony strangely, shaking his head. Something shiny bobbed alongside his jaw. Anthony noted with amazement that the kid had his ears pierced, just like a woman.

"Nah, man," he said. "I'm telling you, Dickinson's Landing and a bunch of other little places—they're long gone. Since before the Seaway opened."

Seaway? Why would the kid make up a story like that? It was an obvious lie, a *pathological* lie. There was something wrong with the kid. Suddenly, Anthony didn't want to be in the car with him anymore. He wanted to be back out in the rain, wet and cold, feeling the mud squirm between his toes. He wanted to be walking, holding his forearm tight against his aching ribs, sloshing one tired foot in front of the other. Cold, hurt and desperate seemed preferable to being in a warm car with this unbalanced stranger.

"You know," Anthony said carefully, "I don't want to be any trouble. I can probably walk the rest of the way now."

The kid looked at Anthony as though he had grown horns. "Are you kidding, dude?" he said. "Listen. I know you want to make that phone call, so once we get up to the highway, you can use my cell. It's just that it's useless until then. No reception. It's a dead zone here."

The pain behind Anthony's eyes grew. "What are you *talking* about?" he asked.

"I'm saying you can use my *phone*," the kid repeated. "Here." He pulled something out of his pocket and jabbed it in Anthony's direction. It appeared to be a rectangular metal case, smaller than a deck of cards. It had a pearlescent finish, like a tiny, expensive casket. But when the kid pushed a button, the thing lit up and flipped open like a switchblade.

Anthony let out a startled cry and shrank against the passenger door. The sudden move made his ribs scream in agony, and his hand flew to his side.

"What the hell?" the kid said. His features had twisted into something sinister. His eyes were wide and his lips were curling down at the corners. He was obviously an evil spirit who wanted nothing more than to take Anthony back to the cemetery. He was reaching out to clutch at him.

No, the kid wasn't clutching—he was pointing—pointing at Anthony's hands. His face was a mask of horror, not evil. Anthony followed the direction of the kid's eyes. He looked down at his own hands, laying cupped in his lap, palms up. They were dark and slick, painted in blood.

"No!" He lifted one hand to inspect it closer and saw that his whole sleeve was soaked in crimson. It was pooling in the small valley where his thighs met, it was trickling down his neck, and he could tell by the coppery smell that now filled the car that it was not rainwater but blood that saturated his hair, his shirt, everything. He touched the spot on his torso where his ribs pained him and felt something slippery and unfamiliar there. When he looked down, glistening loops of intestine were spilling through his fingers.

Anthony looked at the driver one last time. His features were still frozen in terror, and now there was something else—something unreal about him. About everything. The kid was beginning to shimmer like the twisting rivulets of water that ran off the windshield. His image was growing transparent. Anthony squeezed his eyes shut. He was going to pass out, he was sure of it, and he braced himself for the fall...

It was a long, silent fall away from the lights of the car into the utterly silent and complete darkness that he knew so well.

Anthony Knight wasn't sure how long he had been walking when he came upon the cemetery. He knew it was probably only an hour or so, but it seemed like forever. *It's just an old bone yard. No big deal*, he told himself, even as he felt the familiar chill of fear run down his spine. *You know what to do.* And he did know. He simply had to put one muddy foot in front of the other and keep his eyes trained on the road. No matter what happened, he would not look into the cemetery, particularly not when he passed the big granite monument with the elaborately carved armoured knight adorning the top.

Anthony would ignore the cemetery. He would walk, in the rain, for as long as it took, until someone came along to offer him a ride.

The Old Kemper Place

"Steve, we've been living with your parents for three years. They've been good to us, but we need to find our own house," Betty told her husband.

For a moment the man was still and didn't say a word. Then he nodded and reached for his jacket. "You're right. Let's go for a drive right now and see if we can spot something we like."

As the young couple drove along the back roads north of Trenton, they were enjoying the fine weather and each other's company. Steve reached across the car and squeezed Betty's hand. "We'll find a place," he assured her.

She smiled. "I know we will. I really want to start a family. It would be good to be out here in the country. Fresh air is good for children."

"Look, there's a 'for sale' sign propped up against that fence and a house set way back from the road," Steve said, steering the couple's old car into a dirt driveway.

"The place looks pretty rundown," Betty said.

"That might mean it's a bargain," Steve countered, jumping out of the car and running around to open the passenger side door for his wife.

They climbed the rickety steps of the front porch. Betty looked around uneasily while Steve knocked firmly on the door. It creaked open.

"We should leave," Betty cautioned. "We can get the real estate agent's name and drop into his office when we get back to town."

"We're here now, so we might as well look around. If we like the place, we'll go to the guy's office and make him an offer."

"But we're trespassing," Betty protested.

"Maybe so, but we're not going to be disturbing anyone. This house has obviously been abandoned for years. Come on. You're the one who wanted to look for our own place to live in the country. We might have found it, and you won't even come inside."

Betty gave a weak smile, stepped over the threshold and into a room full of furniture. "This is odd," she said, clutching her husband's hand. "It looks as though a family was living here and then just deserted the place."

Steve nodded. "But no one's been here for years, judging by all the cobwebs and dust."

They inched across the creaky floorboards into the darkened living room. The window was broken and a corner of the crocheted curtain fluttered lightly in the breeze, but still the air reeked with decay. Malevolence hung in the air. Betty gagged. Steve reached for her arm. They had to get out of there. "Run!" he shouted, grasping his wife's shoulders to turn her around.

That was when they saw them. A man, a woman and three children staring with sightless eyes, standing motionless—lifeless, like statues. Transparent statues.

Beth and Steve ran to the car, pulled open the doors and locked themselves inside. Neither one said a word. It took several minutes for Steve to calm himself enough to drive, but when he did, he headed straight for the real estate office in town.

"Ah yes," the agent told them with a sigh. "The old Kemper place. We've been trying to sell that property for a dozen or so years now. A dreadful thing, that—murders and a suicide, you know."

The Old Oak Tree

There had always been a very special bond between Kelly and her grandmother, and both of them living in London had only enhanced their connection to one another. They had been there for one another through thick and thin when no one else had been. It had been Grandma who had comforted Kelly when other kids at school had occasionally been mean to her, and Grandma who had patched up the inevitable scrapes and bruises as well. And, although Kelly hadn't known it when she was a child, the support had been mutual. The older woman's relationship with her son, Kelly's father, had always been strained, and the child's presence had brought her grand-mother the comfort of companionship. The two were so close that, on the day of Kelly's wedding, rather than being walked down the aisle by her father, the bride chose to escort her grandmother to a seat of honour before joining Brett, her smiling husband-to-be, at the front of the hall.

But there was another, deeper element of connection between Kelly and her grandmother. Through the years they always seemed to somehow know when something had happened to either one of them. When the girl was in junior high school, Grandma had turned up unexpectedly at the schoolyard gate just as the class bullies had begun to taunt Kelly and her friend. A few months later, the older woman had been on hand to see her granddaughter's entry in the science fair. Kelly had thought it was odd that Grandma had even known about the science fair because as far as the youngster was concerned, entering a project was an extraordinarily uncool thing to do, and she had kept her project a secret. Somehow though, her grandmother had just known.

Again, the connection worked both ways. Kelly couldn't have explained it, but she always just seemed to be aware of her grandmother's moods. It was as if there was a telepathy between them. One day, for instance, Kelly was driving home from work on a rainy day when she suddenly decided to stop at a convenience store. By the time she pulled into the shop's parking lot she couldn't think of anything she wanted to buy, but there she was in front of the store so she bought a small container of cream and took it to her grandmother. When the older woman saw what Kelly had brought, she burst into girlish giggles and told her that she had been wanting a cup of tea all afternoon, but she was out of cream and the rain hadn't let up all day. Kelly knew that their link was vital to them both.

A few months after her wedding, Kelly was delighted to find that she was pregnant. The first person she wanted to tell was Grandma, but she didn't get the chance. The moment Kelly walked into her grandmother's kitchen, the older woman's eyes lit up. "You're going to have a baby, aren't you?" she exclaimed.

"This is one lucky baby, Grandma. He or she will have you to love it…him…her." Kelly laughed.

"I'm going to love that baby with all my heart," Grandma proclaimed. A look passed across her face. "I have to confess, though, something has me feeling uneasy."

"What is it? Just tell me what's making you feel bad, and I'll fix it right away," Kelly promised.

"It's probably nothing—probably just the chatter of an old woman, but dear, I have to tell you, I love that little house of yours, but there's something about that oak tree in the yard that worries me. It seems too close to the house or something. I'm sorry to be a worrywart, but now with the baby coming and all…"

Kelly smiled. "You've mentioned that before, Grandma. I love that old tree, but I promise you that I'll call an arborist first thing tomorrow."

"Thank you, dear," her grandmother said, pouring them each a cup of tea. "Now, tell me how you're feeling; do you think you're going to enjoy being pregnant? It was never in vogue to say so, but I always did enjoy it, you know."

The two chatted for a while longer before Kelly left for home. The next day she kept her promise and called a tree specialist. Before the end of the week, an expert had assured her that the old oak tree in the yard was healthy and should give them many more years of shade and beauty.

Kelly's pregnancy progressed so well that the months seemed to fly by, until one evening her husband noticed that she was limping.

"I know," she replied to his inquiry. "My hip's really sore for some reason. Just the pregnancy, I guess."

The next morning, Kelly woke up with a feeling that something was wrong—not with her or with the baby, but with Grandma. When her grandmother didn't answer the phone, the feeling became stronger. Planning to drive over to her grandmother's house, Kelly had only turned the key in the ignition when her cell phone rang. It was an emergency room nurse calling. Her grandmother had decided to change the bulb in her kitchen light fixture.

She had climbed to the top of a stepstool but had fallen, landing with all her weight on her left hip.

Kelly rushed to the hospital, but from the moment she set eyes on her grandmother lying in the huge metal bed, she knew that the beloved woman's days were numbered —and she was right.

Kelly's mourning was so deep that she couldn't think straight. When labour started at her grandmother's funeral she ignored it at first, thinking it was her grief that was making her uncomfortable. A few hours later, the deceased woman's great-granddaughter was born. The nurses and doctors were amazed at how quiet and almost distracted the new mother had been during the delivery. Of course, they couldn't have known what Kelly saw—the loving apparition of her grandmother hovering close at hand until the baby was born.

Twenty-four hours later, Kelly and Brett came home from the hospital with their new bundle of love. They were still grieving, but now, in addition, both were terrified of the responsibilities ahead. The pre-natal classes had been helpful, but being faced with the reality of caring for a tiny human being was another matter entirely.

When Brett went downstairs to sort some laundry, Kelly paced the hallway outside the baby's bedroom. As she did, a voice echoed down the corridor: "You'll be fine, my dear. The baby is healthy, and you and Brett are capable parents."

"Grandma?" she called to the empty hallway. The soft sound of a girlish giggle was the only response. Kelly sighed, feeling the tension drain from her body.

Two weeks later, Brett had gone back to work and Kelly was alone with her daughter for the first time. The baby was sleeping in the bassinet when Kelly suddenly, inexplicably, felt a veil of sadness settle around her. Crying, she stood up and looked out the window. A sudden gust of wind stirred the bare branches of the old oak tree that her grandmother had been worried about. Seconds later Kelly felt a blanket of warmth envelope her. "You'll be fine, my dear. You're just tired. Lie down and have a nap while the baby is sleeping. I'll be here to watch over you both."

Kelly smiled and curled up in the over-stuffed chair in the baby's room. It was fully two hours later when she woke up to the quiet, cooing sounds of the baby also wakening. All seemed right with the world.

After that incident, Kelly didn't sense her grandmother's presence for more than a year. Then one night the woman's spirit came to her in a dream, beckoning Kelly to follow her into the baby's bedroom. In the dream a terrible storm raged outside. Claps of thunder shook the house, and flashes of lightning lit up the baby's room as though it were midday. Suddenly, with a tremendous crash, a branch from the oak tree crashed through the baby's bedroom window.

Kelly woke up screaming and ran to the baby's room. The child slept peacefully. She glanced out the window. The night was calm and clear. What had made her have such a terrible dream, she wondered, slowly walking back to her own bed.

"It was only a dream," Brett assured her, but try as she might, Kelly couldn't fall back to sleep. Finally she got up and gently picked the baby out of the crib and brought her into bed with them. They all slept soundly until an enormous crash wakened them. A storm had blown up and hurled a branch from the oak tree through the baby's bedroom window. It had landed on the crib.

A Killer Meeting

As always, the staff cafeteria overlooking the Toronto Harbour was crowded and noisy. Cheryl juggled her food tray and scanned the room, looking for her friend Julie.

"Cher! Over here," a voice called from a corner table.

Cheryl smiled and made her way to join Julie. "Thanks for saving me a spot. For a while there it looked like I was going to miss my lunch hour entirely. I couldn't get that last customer off the phone. He placed a good-sized order, though, so at least it'll be worth it on my tally sheet at the end of the month."

"I know what you mean," Julie answered. "Things are slow, aren't they? But who cares? Tomorrow is Saturday."

Both young women smiled at the thought of their plans.

"I'll pick you up at noon and we'll hit every retro shop along Queen West," Julie said.

"By the time we're finished, we'll be the funkiest dressed women at Jason's party. I can hardly wait," Cheryl added as she munched her salad.

Julie nodded. "Me too. It's going to be great, but listen, I have to run right now. My boss called a department meeting, and there's no way I can weasel out of it."

Cheryl started to make a sympathetic remark about the drudgery of meetings, but the words froze in her throat. Were her eyes going wonky? What was wrong? Maybe she'd been hungrier than she'd thought. A frigid coldness penetrated her body. Colour drained from the world around her, leaving everything in sight a sickly grey tone. Things that had been solid and steady just a few seconds ago trembled softly and became ever-so-slightly disjointed. The air buzzed with the sound of hundreds of invisible bees.

Cheryl struggled to choke down the terror-filled confusion surging through her. She glanced toward Julie as a shimmering, iridescent black cloak slowly engulfed her friend. The other woman's face twisted grotesquely and her body had odd, unnatural angles. Cheryl rubbed her eyes. When she opened them the world was filling with colour once again. She had no idea how much time had elapsed. "Julie, what's wrong?" she asked, fighting the panic she felt.

"With me? Nothing, I'm fine," Julie answered, apparently unconcerned. "Actually, I feel better now. The air conditioning was getting to be a bit much, but then a gust of warm air hit me; it felt good. Anyway, like I said, I have to get back to work but I'll see you tomorrow. It'll be a great day. Take care of yourself till then."

Cheryl nodded to her friend. She pushed her chair back, leaving her uneaten lunch on the table, and walked unsteadily back to her spot in the cubicle farm. All afternoon she forced herself to concentrate on work to keep from thinking about the bizarre experience she'd had at lunchtime.

Just before quitting time, Cheryl's boss stepped out of his office. "You've been very quiet this afternoon," he commented.

"Pretty busy, I guess," Cheryl lied.

"Well as long as you're all right," the man said quietly, "because I'm afraid I have some very bad news for you. Something dreadful has happened. Julie Reacher has just died. She was sitting in a department meeting and apparently she had a massive heart attack."

A Super Saturday

"Hurry up, Sam," 13-year-old Randy called to his friend. "The show's starting in less than an hour."

"I can't go," the other boy replied.

"You have to. It's Superman!"

"My bike's broken," Sam announced, solemnly pointing to his CCM Cruiser lying on the lawn beside him.

"We'll thumb a lift then. We can't miss this movie," Randy declared, not realizing—how could he?—that as an adult he would long for the simpler, safer days he had enjoyed as a kid growing up in Hamilton.

The boys hurried to the main street, plastered smiles on their faces to help them look appealing to passing motorists, and stuck their thumbs out to hitchhike. Sure enough, the sixth vehicle that passed them slowed to a stop. The sign on the side of the van read "McClure and Son." Judging by the age of the driver, this man had to be the son.

"Where are you two fellows off to on this fine day?" McClure Junior asked.

"Downtown to the movies," Randy said before adding "sir" as extra insurance to get the ride.

"Hop in then," the young man told them.

"But it says 'no riders' right there on the passenger door," Sam pointed out before Randy had a chance to tell him to keep his mouth shut.

"So don't use the passenger door. Climb in the back door," the man suggested. "It doesn't matter about the 'no riders' policy anymore anyway. My father painted that on the door, and he's been dead for a while now. It's my van; I do what I like."

The two boys scrambled into the back of the van.

"Here we go. Make yourselves comfortable in there, but don't mess around with the packages," the driver told them through a small window in the driver's compartment. "And hold on tight. I have a couple of stops on the way, but I'll have you to the movie theatre in lots of time."

Sam and Randy laughed as the movement of the van cutting in and out of traffic jostled them around with the parcels that McClure Junior had stashed in the back. A few minutes later, the driver pulled to the curb at the top of a hill. "Back in a minute," he told them.

Randy looked out the window in the van's back door. A large truck was pulling in behind the van, and Randy could see that it wasn't going to stop in time. With the two boys captive in the back, the truck smashed into McClure's van and sent the driverless vehicle careening down the hill. The boys screamed in terror. They were headed into traffic—and fast.

"We're gonna get killed!" Sam yelled as he peered through the little window into the empty driver's seat. The world was rushing past them, faster and faster. They were sure to hit something, if not roll over.

Randy scrambled to pull himself up beside Sam. As he did, the steering wheel turned slightly to the left and the van slowed down. "Don't be scared, boys," a disembodied voice told them. "I won't let anything happen to you."

The boys' faces drained of colour. They stared at one another, not knowing whether to be more afraid or less afraid, knowing now that an invisible driver was at the controls.

Sam and Randy watched in horrified fascination as the van swerved around cars and pedestrians. The horn blared over and over again, warning people to get out of the way. Each time the boys heard the horn, they saw the big metal rim inside the steering wheel press down. Someone was holding that steering wheel and honking that horn— someone the two boys couldn't see.

Finally, the van made a wide turn to the left onto a side street and slowed to a stop. The boys banged frantically on the back window until a barber, who had run out of his shop when he heard the commotion on the street, opened the door to free the two badly frightened boys.

An excited crowd gathered around, marvelling at what they had just witnessed—a van that had steered itself to safety. At least one person, however, knew there had been a driver because he'd seen—and recognized—him. It had been none other than old man McClure at the wheel. There was no doubt. The witness had been a good friend of McClure's; he had been a pallbearer at the man's funeral.

Sam and Randy never saw their Superman movie that day. Instead they had had an encounter with the supernatural, a much mightier force than any comic book character.

The Dot Matrix

The house had been a run-down dump when he'd moved into it in 1983, and the past 10 years hadn't been kind, but the place was home and it was where he looked forward to being at the end of every shift. This four-room, two-storey, ramshackle frame house on the outskirts of an industrial area in Timmins had been the first place Vik had lived with anything even approaching contentment.

Of course most of the improvements in Vik's life had nothing to do with the house and everything to do with the fact that five years back he'd finally given up booze. Fear had made him quit—gut-wrenching fear that his drinking would put him in an early grave. By the end, those hangovers were bad—pretty close to life-threatening medical events. But these last years living in the house, alone of course, why they'd been good years, especially since Malcolm had moved in next door.

The two men had bonded from the moment they met. It was comforting to them both to know that neither one had a story that would have shocked the other. After all, if either of them had spent their lives in a sensible, organized way, then neither of them would be living where they did.

Both Malcolm and his house were as run-down as Vik and Vik's house. The two front doors faced each other rather than out onto the street, which was fine with both men because looking out the door at a friend's house was much better than any of the only other views available: ugly concrete walls of half-a-dozen industrial buildings.

The third week in January that year was colder than evil. Friday had Vik working an eight-hour shift in the receiving bay. Every time the shipper had opened the big garage door, an arctic gale had blown straight to Vik's core. He could hardly wait to get home and warm up. The thought of relaxing in his favourite chair watching the Leafs and the Sens duke it out was the only thing that kept him going until quitting time.

But walking into the house later that afternoon was far from the comforting experience he had been anticipating. The radio was turned on, blaring out country and western music. Vik rushed upstairs to the shelf where he kept the cheap little clock radio. He fumbled with a couple of buttons, but nothing stopped the woman's voice from

singing to him at top volume. In frustration, Vik ripped
the cord out of the wall socket and dropped the radio.

His heart thumped against his ribs. What a welcome
home *that* had been. Stupid radio, what would have made
it come on? He never used it—not the radio part anyway
—just the buzzer as an alarm to wake himself up in the
mornings. And even if he had been listening to the radio,
it certainly wouldn't have been a country and western
station. He had never much liked that style of music, and for
a long time now he'd hated it because it reminded him of
his ex-wife. Fortunately Dot was nothing but a bad memory
now, but she had sure caused her share of problems for
him in her day.

Vik left the radio on the floor where he'd dropped it
and went downstairs to get himself something to eat.
A big can of beef stew, that's what he needed. Heat it up,
pour it into a bowl and sit down to see who'd win the
hockey game—Toronto or Ottawa.

Try as he might, though, Vik just couldn't settle. The
racket of that stupid radio blaring echoed in his mind.
The incident even interfered with his regular between-
periods nap because every time he closed his eyes, Dot's
pinched, mean-looking face flashed across his mind.

When he did manage to doze off a bit he woke up
shivering, chilled to the bone. How long had he slept? It
couldn't have been for long; the hockey game was still in
the second period. Vik looked up at the clock—and
screamed. The hands on the old clock, about the only
thing still left from his marriage to Dot, were spinning
around the numbers. It would have looked as though time

was flying, except that the hands were moving backward. He grabbed the clock from the wall and threw it to the floor, breaking it into dozens of pieces.

A shudder ripped through his body. Slowly, balancing himself against the wall, he made his way to the kitchen sink and poured water into his hands and splashed it on his face until the shakes lessened. *Good grief,* he thought. *What's happening? This is worse than the DTs, and I haven't touched a drop for years.* He exhaled the breath he hadn't realized he'd been holding.

Outside, a sudden gust of wind blew and the house moaned, letting icy drafts into its weak spots—sickly, sweet-smelling drafts. Vik whimpered in confusion and fright. *Tired, I'm just tired. I need to go to bed. Things will be all right in the morning.* Thankfully, the man slept soundly all night long.

Saturday dawned clear and cold. Vik hoped that the day off would make his world better. The evening's wind had brought snow overnight, so he'd have to shovel. That would be good; it would give him something to do. He opened the door to breathe in the cold, crisp air.

He was delighted to see Malcolm standing at his own doorway. "Hey there," Vik called out with a chuckle when he saw that his neighbour was also still in his pyjamas.

His friend in the opposite house pulled his housecoat closed at the front and tied its belt in a knot before waving. It was time the two of them got together, Vik thought. After all, it wasn't as though either of them had any pressing engagements—that day or any other—but when he looked again Malcolm had gone back inside and closed his door.

Disappointed, Vik showered and dressed, wondering if he'd somehow offended his friend. Once the thought had crossed his mind, he couldn't shake it loose. Moments later he was obsessing about the possibility that somehow bad feelings had crept into the friendship. That would be unthinkable. He'd have to find out. Besides, he really didn't want to be alone anymore today.

Vik stomped his way through the snow-covered yard between the two houses and knocked on the other man's door. The two chatted amiably at the open door until Malcolm asked, "Don't you need to be getting home?"

"No, why would I have to get home?" Vik asked, puzzled.

The other man laughed and slapped him on the shoulder. "Hey buddy, you can level with me. I'm your friend, right? You can tell me. Besides, I already know—you've had a woman in there since yesterday. I've seen her through the window, a few times actually. She was standing right beside you at the door this morning. That's why I did my housecoat up before I waved to you."

A sound escaped from Vik's throat.

His friend continued. "Hey, before I forget—I saw something on the news last night about a woman walking downtown yesterday and getting hit by a truck. She died before the ambulance even got there. The only reason I mention it is that her name was Dot. That's your ex-wife's name, right? I remember you told me that one time. It's kind of an unusual name, so it stuck in my head."

A Blue Snake

Aaron felt rough—really, really rough. The last decent sleep he'd had was Wednesday night—three days ago.

Thursday evening he'd gone to bed at the usual time and had fallen asleep right away. Half an hour later he was sitting bolt upright in bed, his heart racing from a nightmare. The moment Aaron opened his eyes the dream's details vanished, leaving him with only the merest tendril of a memory, an image—the image of a blue snake.

Shivering, he put on his housecoat and went to the kitchen for a drink of water. He paced back and forth between the sink and the stove trying to shake off the dream's effects, something that might have been easier if he could have remembered what the dream had been about. All he knew was that it had left him feeling extremely uncomfortable—the dream hadn't frightened him, but it had certainly upset him.

Aaron took his glass of water into the living room and turned on the television in time to catch most of the late movie—a disaster flick from the 1980s. He had thought it would bore him to sleep in no time, but it didn't. By 1:30 the movie was over and he was still wide awake.

Rather than lowering himself to watching infomercials, he went back to bed. He tossed and turned for an hour before drifting off to sleep, only to be jolted awake again. He threw off the covers and grabbed the alarm clock. It was 3:07. He couldn't have been asleep much more than half an hour. Sweat poured from his face. That blue snake was there again, this time sliding along a yellow sheet.

It wasn't scary, but it was definitely unsettling because there was an overwhelming sense of responsibility attached to it, as if there was something important that only he could do. But he had no idea what that something was.

Aaron stumbled to the bathroom, turned on the shower and stood under the stream of warm water until the tenant in the apartment below yelled an obscenity through the air duct. Apparently not everyone appreciated his attempt at middle-of-the-night aqua therapy.

A snack—that would help. He would fix himself something to eat. But it didn't help, and by the time he'd finished an oversized peanut butter and jam sandwich, he knew there was no chance he'd be getting back to sleep. He figured he might as well just get dressed and go to work. He could get caught up on paperwork before everyone else arrived for the day. Besides, maybe taking care of the chores he had been neglecting would dissipate this cloud of responsibility that the dream had left him with—to say nothing of the blue snake visual.

By quitting time, Aaron was more than ready to head home. It might be Friday night, but there was no way he was going out. He was just too tired. He would get a good sleep and then be ready for fun on Saturday night—except that just before midnight he was jolted awake by the sound of a man screaming.

Instantly fully awake and standing beside his bed, Aaron realized that it had been his own voice that he heard. That snake again—that stupid blue snake. It was such a bright blue, too bright to be any kind of real snake, slithering along a patch of yellow. What really bothered him, though, was the overpowering sense of responsibility that the dream left him with. It was almost guilt, as if someone were relying on him and he was letting that someone down.

Aaron swore and threw a pillow across the room. This was getting seriously annoying. He'd walked back and forth across his bedroom floor a dozen times before he realized that he was nowhere near being calmed down enough to go back to sleep. Warm milk, that would help. Waiting for the saucepan to heat, it occurred to Aaron that dreams were supposed to be meaningful, weren't they? Was his subconscious mind trying to tell him something? If that something was so important, why wouldn't his mind let him remember the whole dream instead of just the infernal blue snake?

Aaron turned on the television. An informercial. It didn't matter, it was just something to keep his mind off the dream while he drank the warm milk. He sat cupping the warm mug in his hand with the volume on the TV turned down low. He hadn't even realized that he'd fallen asleep until he heard the mug crash to the floor. "Stupid blue snake!" he screamed at the smiling hucksters still on the screen.

He poured himself a shot of brandy, downed it and poured a second. This had to stop. He needed to get some sleep. Why was he having that dumb dream? What would make him dream about a snake, and why would it make him feel so responsible?

Aaron looked at the full shot glass and realized he'd better go back to bed because if he didn't, he would effectively be drinking first thing in the morning and that just couldn't be a good sign. Besides, it was Saturday; he could sleep in a bit and still enjoy his day off.

But as it turned out, he couldn't sleep at all. Aaron spent Saturday in a sleep-deprived daze. By evening he poured himself a stiff drink, passed out on the couch and stayed there—until the recurring dream jolted him awake once again. Still the blue snake! What was it? What could a blue snake on a yellow sheet possibly mean?

When Aaron realized he was on the verge of crying, he poured himself another drink. By the time the sun came up, he was bleary eyed and knew for certain that there was no hope of salvaging anything of the weekend. It was gone. Shot. Thanks to a stupid nightmare. Now he had to face the reality of going back to work the next day having had almost no sleep since Wednesday night.

He had never been much for physical exercise, but he was desperate. He laced up his sneakers and walked as fast as he could to the shores of Lake Couchiching. The view of the lake lifted Aaron's spirits so much that it occurred to him that this was not only exactly what he should be doing right now, but also exactly where he belonged. He broke into a leisurely jog. Now he felt even better. *Maybe all of these weekend warriors are onto something*, he thought.

The trails would be crowded later on in the morning, but right now they were empty and peaceful. Aaron picked up the pace. This was downright exhilarating! He was going to run the blue snake and the free-floating anxieties right out of his mind. Wonderful! He pushed himself to go faster, until he heard something—or at least he thought he had heard something.

He had. He had heard something. It was a kid's voice crying for help.

Aaron scanned the horizon, but there was nothing to see. Maybe the lack of sleep had made his ears play tricks on him. But no, there was a boat or a raft or something floating out there. He looked around frantically, hoping there was someone nearby who would know what to do, but the beach was deserted. In a couple of hours there would be lots of people here, but for now he was alone, with a choice to make—swim out there or pretend he hadn't heard the voice.

He couldn't, just couldn't ignore the voice. Someone was in serious trouble, and he was the only one who could help. Adrenaline surged through Aaron as he kicked off his sneakers and raced for the lake. "Hang on!" he yelled, but a wave splashed over his head and stole his voice.

Minutes later, his arms ached from the cold and the strain of pulling against the choppy water. He paused, treading water and looking around to get his bearings. He was close enough that he could see a child waving from an inflatable boat. Aaron willed his arms and legs to keep pushing him forward.

When he looked up again, he was close enough to grab the blue rope snaking along the side of the bright yellow dingy.

"Help me, help me, please help me," a little girl inside the boat pleaded.

"Gotcha now," Aaron assured the child as he grasped the blue nylon rope firmly in his right hand and slowly but steadily began the long swim back to the safety of the shore. A feeling of relief coursed through his veins. He'd done it! He had saved a child's life, and it had all gone so smoothly that it felt as though he had rehearsed it.

The two seemingly random human beings—a child whose life was in jeopardy and a young man who had been having nightmares—were safely on the beach. Finally the dream made sense, with its sense of urgent responsibility and the blue rope encircling the yellow boat like a snake. He had dreamt it over and over until he was prepared for the rescue. But how could he have known that this child would need his help? What had caused that dream? Aaron wasn't a religious man, but he did wonder about divine intervention. The only other possibility he could think of—that his subconscious mind had slipped ahead through a tiny tear in the fabric of time—was too freaky to contemplate for long.

On Sunday night, Aaron slept like a baby.

Tied to the End

Mary's jaw tightened as she glared at her nephew, her eyes shining with rage. "I won't hear of it. You mustn't see Judith again. That woman's beneath you and you know it. You were raised to expect better, Paul—much better. She's nothing more than a servant. No good will come of it if you pursue a relationship with her, you mark my words…"

Paul wanted to point out that Judith was a private-duty nurse for the wealthiest family in Cornwall, hardly a position that could be classified as "a servant," but he held his tongue. Anything he said would only prolong his aunt's tirade. It was sad. Aunt Mary was still young and healthy. She could be busy and enjoying her life, but she had always been a snob and ridiculously protective of her nephew. He had been orphaned as a baby and she had taken him in. With each passing year she had clung on to him more and more desperately until, by now, her behaviour was frightening, bordering on insanity. Something would have to be done about the situation soon, but, for the moment, he simply needed to escape from her irrationality.

"I've had enough," he said quietly before walking down the hall and away from the woman's increasingly shrill rant.

Even through his closed his bedroom door, Paul could hear the familiar sounds of Aunt Mary throwing carefully chosen objects against a wall or on the floor. He knew from experience that her temper tantrums were only attention-getters. She never smashed anything of value—only specifically chosen trinkets that she collected at yard sales.

Disheartened, Paul shook his head. In her way Aunt Mary had been good to him, but this pattern couldn't continue. He couldn't let his aunt and her unreasonable behaviour interfere with the relationship that was building with Judith. He liked her so much—or was it actually love he was feeling? There was definitely that possibility.

He had to do something, and he would—in the morning. Tonight he would take just the absolute necessities and slip out through his bedroom window. He'd stay in the old hotel at the edge of town. By morning Aunt Mary would have calmed down and he could begin to investigate options for both of them. For now he would leave a note letting her know where he was staying and that she shouldn't worry. As his feet touched the ground outside, a wave of relief swept over him. He knew there were complications ahead, but he'd deal with them one at a time.

In his car, Paul continued to ponder his situation. Once he could be certain that Aunt Mary was going to be all right, Paul could make his own decisions and plans and just let his relationship with Judith blossom slowly. He knew it would take a long time for him to recover from all the years of living with his aunt's tyrannical rule, and he didn't want either Judith or himself to be hurt any further. Tonight at least he'd get a peaceful night's sleep—even if it was in a rundown hotel.

The room was barely adequate—a double bed, a small television and a bedside table with a phone on it. None of that mattered; he had the place to himself, and that was a relief. No one would be screeching in his ear.

Paul lay down on the bed, and seconds later he was asleep. He was so deeply asleep that it took him several moments to realize that the noise he was hearing wasn't in his dream. Someone was knocking at the door. No, not just knocking. Pounding.

He struggled groggily to the door. Judith! She was barefoot, her jacket was ripped and her hair dishevelled.

What was that around her neck? He had given Aunt Mary that scarf for Christmas. Why would Judith be wearing it? Why was it all ripped and crooked like that?

"Judy, come in," he said putting his arm around the young woman and gently pulling her into the room before closing the door. "What's happened? How did you find me here?"

Her only answer was to slump heavily into Paul's arms.

"You're so cold, Judy. How long have you been outside? Never mind that now, there's a thick blanket on the bed and you'll warm up in no time. We'll talk in the morning. For now, just rest." Paul tucked the sheets and blankets around the young woman before lying down beside her, hoping that his body heat would help to warm her.

He slept fitfully through the night, dreaming one strange dream after another. The only one he could remember, the last one, was something about bright red tulips blooming on icebergs. Then the tulips became bells, and they rang in a lovely light tone—at first. Then they rang louder and their sound was harsh, horribly harsh. Paul whimpered in his sleep and pulled the pillow over his head to muffle the hideous noise. The iceberg was making him cold, dreadfully cold.

Slowly wakefulness penetrated his tormented mind. There was no iceberg, no red tulips, no bells. The phone beside his bed was ringing and the blankets were all on the floor. Paul was colder than he could ever remember being. His nearly frozen fingers fumbled with the phone.

"Paul Billingsley?" a man's voice asked.

Paul propped himself up on his elbow and mumbled into the phone.

"It's the front desk calling. There's an OPP constable here for you. They need you down at the station right away."

"Police?" Paul mumbled, rubbing the back of his hand across his eyes as if hoping the movement would help him understand what was happening.

"It's your aunt, sir. She's been arrested; something about strangling a neighbour's nurse."

The iceberg from his dream ground into Paul's stomach and the shabby hotel room spun. Aunt Mary? That was ridiculous. She was at home where he had left her. But Judith? Where was Judith? She had been here in this room, he knew she had. He remembered it all very clearly, especially because she'd been wearing his aunt's scarf.

Or wait. Did he just dream that?

No. Judith *had* been here, and there on the pile of blankets beside the bed was Aunt Mary's scarf—the one that had been wrapped around Judith's neck at such an odd angle.

Just Joking

"They've done a great job on this place," Brent said to his girlfriend Nicole as they walked into the freshly renovated Thunder Bay restaurant and pub.

"You've been here before?" Nicole asked.

The man nodded. "Last year a bunch of us dropped in here after a football game. What a rundown dump. The place is so old that my grandfather and his friends used to hang out here when they were young. Joe, the original owner, would even let them sneak in a game of poker now and again."

"Those days are sure gone. Someone has spent a fortune here, and I guess anyone who wanted to play poker these days would just go online," Nicole added.

"Check this out," Brent said, pointing to a weather-beaten sign in a glass cabinet next to the foyer. "It's good they saved that old wooden sign."

Nicole squinted at the cracked plank of wood with its faded red paint spelling out "Joker's Wild" across the top, and below, in black paint, an arrow pointed to the dining room named "King's Table." She shivered. "Can we go inside now? There's an awful draft coming from somewhere," Nicole urged.

Brent nodded. "Let's sit at the table in the far corner, if we can. That was the one my grandfather and his friends practically owned."

Once they were seated, they each opened their menus and gave the items a cursory glance. Nicole closed hers first and said, "We're at a pub—might as well treat ourselves to some pub grub, at least for an appetizer."

The nachos and cheese were the best they'd ever eaten.

"Yum. That was delicious," Brent said, wiping his fingers on a large paper napkin.

Nicole nodded. "Good food, definitely. I hope the new owner does well, especially as he's gone to so much trouble to respect the building's history. You know, preserving that old decrepit sign and keeping the original names."

"It's bad luck to change a name, I think," Brent commented. "Especially here."

"Why's that?" Nicole asked.

"My grandfather told me that the man who started the business had quite an ego. He even subtly named the place after himself. His name was Joe King, so that's why the pub is called Joker's Wild and the restaurant is called King's Table.

Nicole laughed. "That was pretty darned clever!"

"There's quite the story about the sign, too."

"Well, we're here and you've told me this much, so you'd better tell me about the sign."

Brent smiled and took a sip of his drink. This was a tale he had grown up hearing. "Remember I said that Joe had an ego? Well, when he had that sign painted, he had a picture of himself painted in the centre of it."

"He was vain, wasn't he?" Nicole shivered a bit and pulled her coat around her shoulders.

Brent nodded. "After Joe died, his friends held a wake for him here in the pub. It was a bad night—rainy and cold—but my grandfather and his buddies came to pay their respects. They decided it would be fitting to have a quick round of blackjack in honour of their old friend. My grandfather swears that as the cards were dealt he looked up and saw Joe, well his spirit at least, drenched with rain, standing by the table. Gramps didn't say anything to anyone because he didn't want his friends to think he was crazy, but the image upset him so much that he left the wake right away. It was pouring rain by then, just a miserable night. As my grandfather was walking to his truck, he looked back toward the pub to see if anyone else was leaving and might need a drive home. As he did, he noticed something very strange about the sign."

Nicole leaned forward and signalled Brent to continue.

He lowered his voice. "The picture of Joe had just disappeared."

"That's just a tall tale, a bunch of hokum your grandfather made up to—" A sudden blast of cold air silenced her.

Traces of anger stirred in Brent's gut. He wasn't going to let Nicole dis his family's legend or spoil his meal. He reached for his menu again. Two playing cards fell from inside the menu as a shawl of cold, damp air settled heavily around Nicole's shoulders. They stared at the cards on the table—a joker and a king.

Rescued

Brian clung to the overturned boat, his fingers cramping from the cold. Terror, anger and confusion cascaded over him. How could he have been so stupid as to get himself into this mess? No time for that now, though. He could berate himself later—maybe. Right now he needed to concentrate on something much more important: saving his own life. He was alone, clinging to a small, capsized motorboat somewhere in Georgian Bay. He'd lived near the South Channel all his life, and he knew that there was nothing good about his situation.

Waves poured over him, harder and higher. Worse, he was losing his grip—on the gunnel and on his emotions. "Idiot," Brian chastised himself, struggling to get a firmer hold. "Even talking to yourself now. Not a good sign."

But a small part of his brain took solace in the one-sided conversation. At least he was still rational enough to realize what a mess he was in. "If I was totally hypothermic, I'd be too confused to know I was acting crazy."

A swell of lake water hit him in the face as he tried to take a breath. "Don't panic, man. Someone will come to get you," he tried to reassure himself in a barely audible voice. "They'd better move it. I can't hold on much longer."

Brian laid his head on the nearly submerged bow and cried from pain, frustration and terror. Was it even worth trying to hold on? He was going to die anyway. Why not just get it over with, simply let go and slip into the icy depths below…

Was that a noise? Maybe just the sound of his own sobs. Or something else? A rescue boat? Brian's hopes soared. He looked around at the cold, black water that surrounded him. It was impossible to make out where the water ended and the sky began. Maybe there isn't any sky, he mused illogically before realizing that his flawed attempt at reasoning was a bad sign.

But he *could* hear something. He was sure of it. He scanned the horizon as best he could. There was something! Not just an ordinary something, either. There was a ship's engine, and it was coming his way. Brian had lived on the shore of this bay all his life. He knew what a boat looked and sounded like from a distance, and yes, definitely, there *was* a ship approaching—a good sized one.

He tried to wave toward his potential rescuers, but his arm wouldn't move. *It's okay*, he told himself. *They'll see me.* And with that comforting thought, Brian drifted into unconsciousness.

"Are ya in there, lad?" A voice pierced the haze of sleep but from so far away that Brian knew he'd have to yell his answer, and he didn't have that kind of strength right now. He let himself drift back into the blissful abyss of unconsciousness.

Sometime later, Brian opened his eyes—but he couldn't see. His hands flew to his face. What was wrong? His eyes were certainly open. *I'm blind*, he thought, until tiny pinpoints of light came into focus. His vision was fine. It was night, a dark, moonless night. There was nothing to see. Brian realized that he was still outside, but at least he wasn't in the water anymore. He was lying on a ship's deck staring up at a clear, star-filled sky.

Slowly the rest of his senses kicked in. He could feel the ship riding the waves and hear water hitting against the sides. He struggled to prop himself up to a sitting position but only managed to barely lift his shoulders. If boats hadn't been part of his life forever, Brian might not have recognized his surroundings. As it was, though, he knew he was aboard a replica of an old lake steamer.

Then the blissful awareness that he'd been rescued sunk in. He lay back down and soon lost consciousness again.

"Laddie!" someone called. It was the same voice as before—closer this time, though. Could he muster the strength to answer?

"You saved me," Brian whispered to the man standing over him.

"Aye laddy, we did. Nothing terrible can happen to you now. You're as safe as you can be. Just rest now, you hear?"

"Can you spare some water?" he asked his caretaker.

The older man pulled at a strap slung over his shoulder until an old metal canteen appeared. He unscrewed the lid and handed the dented container to Brian, who managed to prop himself up on an elbow. He drank greedily.

"Whoa there, mate. Take sips or you'll make yourself sicker than you already are."

Grudgingly, Brian forced himself to lower the water bottle away from his lips. He eased himself up to a sitting position and looked around. He was inside a cabin now. Waves slapped against the brass-rimmed porthole beside his bunk. It was pretty obvious that he hadn't been rescued by any ordinary vessel. This was one realistic restoration job for sure—not a scrap of fibreglass or vinyl to be seen. She had to be either a beautifully redone classic or a carefully, and expensively, handcrafted new boat.

He noticed that someone had decorated the opposite wall of the cabin with an old-fashioned lifesaver ring. Nice touch, except why would a boat-owner decorate his craft with the name *Waubuno*? That old ship was a legend around these parts. Whoever owned this rig was clearly a sicko, but at least Brian was safe now. There was plenty of time to let the harbour authorities know about this mariner's disrespect to the two dozen people who had lost their lives aboard the *Waubuno* when she went down in 1879. It was just tasteless to mock such a tragedy.

He was slipping back to sleep when he realized that the same man was standing beside him again. It was weird how quietly this dude walked. Brian hadn't heard the guy approach or even open the cabin door. He tried to prop himself up on his elbow to get a good look at this turkey so that he could identify him later. It was tough, though. Brian's body felt so heavy—strangely heavy. Was he still that weak from his ordeal?

"Don't struggle, my young friend. I just came to check on you. As you can see, you've been rescued by the *Waubuno*. I'm her captain, Burkett is my name. When you can, let me know what to call you."

Evil

In a darkened room, a man sat hunched over a table, waiting for deliverance to ooze through his pen, onto the sheet of paper that lay before him. No one would ever read the words he wrote. He simply needed to purge the evil from his mind, clear it from his body.

Imperceptibly at first, his pen quivered. Then the slight movement became more obvious, but even so, drops of sweat from his forehead stained the paper before the ink did.

He rubbed his eyes. His mind was a black, swirling mass. He tried not to think. When the pen did move across the paper, he was surprised to see that he had actually written a word: "Evil," an anagram for vile…

As teenagers, Alexander and his friends had spent many long, deliriously happy summer days at the shore of Lake Ontario where it lapped up against the quaint community of Oakville. The town had been sparsely populated then, mostly by wealthy folk whose palatial houses rarely seemed to be occupied. Of course progress was inevitable, but still, Alex had felt a stab of nostalgia when developers announced they were buying up the old lakefront properties. No doubt there'd soon be a herd of bulldozers lumbering over the landscape, crushing the manicured gardens that surrounded those once-grand mansions.

The odd thing was that he'd always been pretty sure that one of those big houses belonged to a relative of his—an aunt—his father's sister, Edith. He'd never met the woman. Her name was rarely uttered in his family's home, and the reason for the estrangement was certainly never up for discussion. Still, it was a surprise to read in the *Spectator* that she was the only person who had refused to sell her home, no matter how much money the construction companies offered her.

"Vile old coot. Vengeful. Always was," Alex's father muttered before dropping the newspaper on a chair and leaving for work.

Her letter to Alex arrived the next day. He opened the envelope and stared at the spidery handwriting on the expensive vellum notepaper. A foul taste soured his mouth. Edith's message was straightforward: her house, everything in it and the land it stood on were his, free and clear—if he followed her directives. The note concluded, "Alexander, go to my house immediately. Go alone. All further necessary actions will become clear then."

Should he phone his father? No, it would just upset the man. This was something Alex had to do on his own.

He parked the car at the address she'd given him and walked up to the old house. When there was no response to his knock, he turned the doorknob; the door swung open, and he walked in. An odd sense of detachment descended around him. He had never seen a dead body before, nor had he ever met his aunt, but still he knew that the elderly woman in the long, satin gown, lying peacefully on the sofa, was his father's estranged sister. He also knew that she was dead and probably had been for two days, the same number of days it had taken for her letter to get to Alex.

The sourness he'd tasted upon opening her letter now permeated the air. He had to get out of here. No one ever had to know that he had been here. Go back home now. Think this through. Options, there are lots of options. Alex bolted for the open door and its promise of freedom and fresh air. As he reached for the handle, a putrid cloud slammed the door closed.

"No!" a voice from somewhere, nowhere, everywhere, ordered.

He leaned against the doorjamb, the periphery of his vision pulsing with circles of bright lights. He was going to faint. *A drink, I need a drink.* He stumbled to the dining room and grasped a decanter from the table. The amber liquid burned his throat before mixing in his bloodstream to soften some of the jagged edges.

He needed to think, but all he could do was feel. He could feel death in the air, that was certain, but there was something far worse than that here as well. There was evil. Waves of foul-smelling air pulsed through the house, so strong he could barely stand against them.

Another envelope with the same cramped writing lay on the silver tray beside the decanter. Alex opened it. "I left this note here because I knew you would need a drink. Finally I have found the perfect vengeance against my brother. I have his son."

A Dream that is Not

In Guelph, on a cold December night in 1962, a small boy wearing flannelette pyjamas huddled at the top of the staircase barely daring to breathe. At the bottom of the staircase, his parents were hosting a Christmas party. They'd given him a bottle of pop, a plate of treats and strict instructions to stay upstairs in his bedroom. He hadn't touched either the food or the drink, nor had he stayed in his bedroom. Instead he had turned all his attention to eavesdropping on the adults' conversations.

One man's voice rose above the din. "I'll tell you, Jack, I would never want to go through that again. I don't mind telling you that I was scared stiff."

The boy shivered at the thought that something could be so frightening that it would scare an adult.

Downstairs there were murmurs of response before the voice continued. "I'd just cleared Trenton, heading toward Belleville. I won't take the 401, not at night anyway, so it was a bit slow going. But what did I care? The boss was paying mileage and overtime. Anyway, I noticed the bushes at the side of the road moving a bit, like there might be an animal in there. I slowed down a bit more in case a deer was going to jump out on the road in front of my car."

The storyteller paused. Judging from the cloud of smoke that wafted up the stairs to the child's perch, the man had stopped talking to light a cigarette.

"Well, a second later there sure as heck was something in front of my car, but it wasn't a deer. I'd have welcomed the sight of a deer once I realized what it was there on the road just ahead of me. It was a team of horses pulling an old-fashioned stagecoach! I'm telling you, it was an actual stagecoach."

The room downstairs was getting more and more quiet. The little child wasn't the only one listening to this tale.

"I slammed on the brakes so hard that the rear end of my car fishtailed. Even so there was no chance I'd miss them. But it was the darndest thing. I didn't hit them. I drove straight through them, the coach and the horses. Obviously I knew right then and there that there was something unnatural about this whole thing. All of a sudden, getting to Belleville that evening just didn't matter. I swung the car around, headed back toward Trenton and checked into the first flea-bag motel I could find."

The partiers were so quiet now that the boy held his breath for fear they'd hear him.

"I slammed a 10-dollar bill on the counter at the front desk and told the fellow that I needed a room for the night. He could tell I was upset, that was for sure, because he asked me if there was anything wrong. Well I wasn't about to tell some stranger that I'd just seen a phantom stagecoach pulled by phantom horses, so I just shook my head. He knew though; you could see it in his eyes. He hummed and hawed a bit but finally told me what he knew. It seems that every year on October 4th, he gets someone checking in just about the same time. They're always driving on Highway 2, trying to make it through to Belleville for the night, when a pair of horses pulling a stagecoach appears on the highway right in front of their eyes. He said I looked so shaken up that he figured that was exactly what had happened to me. I just shook my head, took the room key and walked away."

Shivering, the small boy made his way to the comfort of his bedroom. Downstairs the din of conversation picked up once again.

By breakfast time the next morning, the blessing of sleep had erased the story from the child's conscious mind, and the memory would no doubt have stayed buried in his unconscious, perhaps confused as a dream, except for a comment his mother made as she poured coffee into his father's mug: "We'll not be taking Highway 2 after dark again anytime soon. That was some terrifying experience Chris had, wasn't it?"

The child shuddered, knowing that it hadn't been a dream.

The Plan

"Listen up, 'gels!"

Max always talked like that, kind of rough. No one ever took any offense, though; it was just a leftover rough spot from when he'd been physical. He'd been one bad dude, or at least that's what I've been told—a petty thug, a drug dealer and a big time biker. Not a nice guy, anyway, and apparently he'd been furious when his Harley went for its fateful skid on the 400 and he came flying off the bike, smack into the grill of a semi going the other way, only to find himself here. I don't know firsthand, of course, because I wasn't even here then, but I'm guessing that's why he's a bit gruff. You get used to it pretty quick because these morning meetings are mandatory. Plus, I mean he has a boss too, you know, so he has quotas to fill, and there *are* a lot of us to supervise: an entire choir.

In case you're not familiar with the term, it doesn't mean we sing, it's just the word for a group of angels—a choir—like a murder of crows or a pride of lions. We're a choir of angels.

Anyway, Max cleared his throat and you could've heard a pin drop—even on the cloud we were all standing on. "You need to hear this. It's crucial that it happens today in Haliburton," Max informed us. "Administration made it clear that exactly a year from today, one of the really extraordinary ones needs to be born."

"Hey," Samuel called out. "I thought we were supposed to believe that all morts were extraordinary."

Max looked exasperated but continued. "Yeah, well, that's administration's line, but you know as well as I do that some morts are more extraordinary than others. But never mind that right now. We have a challenge ahead of us because, as of this moment in mortal time, the parents of that extraordinary little being haven't even met."

A chorus of moans echoed among us.

"It's going to take a good team to get this thing done in a timely manner. An experienced pair who know how to work the angles. Any volunteers?" Max asked. Then, without pausing for as much as a breath, let alone an answer, he hollered, "Bert and Mandy, this one is yours. I've got a stat sheet here for you, but don't get bogged down by the details. Remember, this one's urgent. I need you to do me proud, folks. Shake a leg. The future of the human race is resting on your performance."

The rest of the choir began to shimmer until their energy scattered into the ether. Just Mandy and I were left on the cloud. I knew it wasn't cool to be enthusiastic about an assignment, especially not an urgent one, but frankly I always get a kick out of mingling with the morts. Mandy and I nodded at one another—partners.

Jordan scrunched up the sheets of paper he'd been reading and cursed the stuffy air in his apartment. He had to get outside even if he hadn't accomplished anything all day. Well, actually he hadn't accomplished anything all week. He yelled in exasperation and punched the cushions on the couch. He shouldn't go out. He should stay right here in his solitary confinement and keep trying to write. He'd given himself two weeks to draft the novel he'd spent years wanting to write, and he'd been holed up in his apartment for six days already, but nothing—not one idea—had come to him. He was frustrated, disappointed and overwhelmed with loneliness.

I'll go for a walk. A walk always helps. He scowled as he slipped on his shoes and stepped out into the corridor. He knew he was in a foul humour, but when he caught a glimpse of his reflection in the mirrored elevator doors he did a double take. He couldn't go out anywhere, not even just for a walk, looking as bad as he did right now.

Jordan went back into his apartment, shaved, showered and put on fresh clothes. *I should've done that first thing this morning. Maybe isolating myself isn't as good an idea as I thought it was. I'm definitely going for a walk.*

Mandy reached over and tugged at one of my wing feathers. She winked and whispered, "Nice touch."

Emma shoved her stethoscope into her lab coat pocket. She needed to get outside, to get away from people. It had been a long and gruelling shift, but that was what a career in emergency medicine was all about, and she knew it. What hurt was being surrounded by people all the time and yet still feeling so achingly lonely.

As she walked through the automatic doors into the ambulance bays, someone called her name. For a split second it crossed her mind to pretend that she hadn't heard the voice, but just for a moment.

"Dr. Thornton!" the voice repeated. "I'm glad I caught you. We need you in the plaster room."

Emma nodded and walked back into the hospital knowing that this was precisely why she had chosen this career. Here was another chance to make a difference.

I leaned toward Mandy. We hovered, invisibly of course, a few metres above street level. "We are so good at this," I told her with pride.

"Well, Max gave us good background," she said, practicing that humility we're supposed to be striving toward.

Jordan swung his arms as he strode along the busy sidewalk. He breathed deeply and realized how much he was enjoying the sensation of being jostled by the crowds. Even the noise and the smell of the traffic energized him. He hadn't felt this good for days. The more he walked, the more he felt like walking. It was wonderful.

Before he knew it, the young man was a long way from his apartment and equally as far away from his self-centred troubles. There was a café on the corner. Judging by its steamy windows the place was crowded, but that didn't matter to Jordan. He suddenly wanted very much to be a part of that crowd, enjoying a muffin and a steaming cup of strong coffee.

"You'll be as good as ever in no time," Emma said as she lifted the little boy down from the examining table.

Now I'm going to make sure I get away for coffee, Emma thought as she erased her name from the "on shift" section of the white board hanging in the hospital corridor.

As she approached the door to the café, she realized the tiny restaurant was so crowded that she'd have to line up to buy a coffee. *It'll be worth the wait,* Emma decided as she reached for the door handle.

Jordan pulled the café door open and held it for an attractive woman. "After you," he smiled.

"Thanks," Emma mumbled, scanning the shop's small interior and wondering if she was going to find a table. There was always the option of walking back to the hospital and grabbing a cup of coffee from the cafeteria.

"I see a table and two chairs over there in the corner," Jordan said.

Was that man talking to her?

"If you go and hold that table, I'll bring us some coffee and a snack," Jordan offered.

He was talking to her. Should she brush him off? It'd have to be politely, though. The guy certainly hadn't done anything offensive. Besides, he had a nice look about him, like someone she'd enjoy getting to know. She smiled and said, "All right."

Had that cosy café not been so noisy with espresso machines hissing, coffee cups clattering and people talking, the morts might have thought they heard bells ringing. Really it was just Mandy and me congratulating each other on a job well done.

We fluffed our wings and were off to file our report before the afternoon meeting.

Chapter 2: First Quarter

Past Falls

Amy smiled. She'd have the whole day to herself. Her friends were pumped about their cross-border shopping expedition, but all she really wanted was some down time; the trip to Niagara Falls was just a bonus. She really should have stayed behind at the dorm to study, but a bit of a drive from London for a change of scenery didn't mean she couldn't study. It might even be quieter here than in the residence, and besides, when she needed a break from the books she'd have the spectacle of Niagara Falls with all its chaos and fun.

After three hours of poring over a physiology textbook, Amy badly needed a break. Out on the sidewalk in front of her hotel she looked around. What would be the craziest thing to do? Should she take the elevator to the top of the viewing tower? Catch a show at the water park, or maybe even scare herself in one of the mocked-up haunted houses? Choosing wasn't easy and she did need to do a lot more studying, but she wanted to have something to tell her friends about because they'd certainly have mounds of stories for her about finding designer clothes at rock-bottom prices.

Amy squinted into the bright sunshine and wondered if she could ever live here. The place was always so crowded and noisy. Of course, even without the crowds it would still be noisy because, as any high school physics course would have taught, that volume of water dropping from such great a height is going to create one thundering big noise.

Amy stood at the edge of the hotel's lawn. She closed her eyes and concentrated on just hearing the sound of the waterfalls. After a while she could do it—block out everything except the roaring noise of the falling water. What a strange sensation! It was sort of like hearing history because that roar had been going on since the land had been formed. She felt like she had years ago in a funhouse at the CNE. Dizziness and a strange sound made her open her eyes. There was a dilapidated bus on the street right in front of her. Strange. The other tour buses around here were shiny and new.

"Come on up, little lady," the driver said, waving her on the bus.

Little lady? she thought. *What kind of a tacky phrase is that?* Still, Amy hadn't thought of anything better to do, so she pulled some change of out her jacket pocket and looked around for a fare box. "Should I have bought a ticket?" she asked the driver.

"This is what they call a courtesy tour, ma'am. As a matter of fact, we give *you* a coin, a souvenir coin," the driver explained, and handed her a silver token about the size of a loonie.

"Thanks," Amy mumbled in confusion. What had ever made her think that riding a tour bus in Niagara Falls was going to be a good idea? It was too late to change her mind now, she realized, watching the driver crank the door closed. He had quite the get-up on—very old-fashioned. It was obviously a costume of some sort. He was all decked out like a picture in a history book, maybe someone from the last century.

Amy found an empty seat and turned to look out the window. Things looked pretty weird out there—beyond weird, actually—so strange that it took a moment for her to realize where she was and what was happening. This wasn't a really old bus; this was a rolling theatre made to *look* like an old-fashioned bus. Even the windows weren't really windows. They had to be screens—plasma screens showing computer generated images of what the area would have looked like in the 1920s. *Bizarre, but I'm here now; I might as well enjoy it*, she thought.

Beautiful green lawns, stately three-storey brick houses and couples dressed in old-fashioned clothing rolled by. Mildly intrigued, Amy decided to play along with the bus company's idea of a historic tour. Of course she knew the whole thing was a bit of a hoax, but it was fun in a campy sort of way, and she really didn't want to make a scene by asking to get off the bus.

The other people on the bus were every bit as odd as the driver, so they probably worked for the company too. At least the attention to detail was impressive. Every now and again there'd even be a shot of an antique car driving by.

The whole scene was quiet and peaceful, especially compared to the constant hustle and bustle around Niagara Falls these days. Just as Amy had settled in to enjoy herself, she felt the bus slow down and pull over to the curb. The show was obviously over, but even that part had been so realistically done that now Amy was actually sorry to leave. Still, she did have to study, especially if she wanted to join her friends for a bit of a pub crawl this evening.

"I hope you enjoyed the tour, miss," said the driver. "Hang on to that coin. You never know, it might be worth something one day."

"Thanks," Amy said. She'd forgotten about the souvenir. She took it out of her pocket as she walked along the crowded sidewalk. It was heavy and very detailed. Not much of a surprise from whatever company had put that supposed historic bus tour together. There was an image of the falls on one side of the coin and a man's head on the other. The thing was really quite impressive. Those didn't look like stamped images; they actually looked as though they'd been engraved. Maybe the driver knew what he was talking about when he told her to save it. For now she simply put the token back in her pocket.

Back in the hotel room, Amy made herself as comfortable as she could with her textbook. And that was exactly where her friends found her two hours later—fast asleep with her cheek pressed against an illustration of the human knee joint.

"Wake up!" all three yelled at once. "If you were just going to sleep, you should have come with us. We had a great time."

Amy stretched and sat up. "Did you get some bargains?"

"We didn't buy a thing. We didn't even leave Niagara Falls. The line-up at the border crossing was way too long so we came back into town and did every touristy thing there is to do. We went up the viewing tower, rode the rides, went through the museums and even took in a haunted house. It was all just as much fun as it was when we came here with our parents when we were kids. It was great. Honestly, you should have come with us. It was a lot of fun."

"Good," was the only response Amy could manage as the memory of her own afternoon's adventure floated into her consciousness. Maybe she'd just fallen asleep and dreamt it all.

But there, lying on her book, was an engraved silver coin.

"Hey, where did you get that? We saw one just like it in one of the museums we went through. They used to hand them out on a bus tour around the falls way back in the 1920s. They're really valuable now. Can you believe that?"

Amy swallowed hard. What the heck had happened to her? Had she walked into some sort of time warp? No, of course not. There was no such thing. Still, she knew that the question of where she had gotten the coin would be impossible to explain—even to herself.

A Long, Cold Walk

"Who the dickens would be pounding on my door at this time of night?" Ken grumbled. For a moment he debated not answering the door. He was watching a re-run of *Rockford Files* and it was one of his favourite episodes, but his curiosity got the best of him and he eased himself out of his tattered recliner.

Ken had chosen the location for his house very carefully. It was well north of Richmond Hill but still a bit south of

Aurora and a good distance in from Yonge Street. His driveway was almost a kilometre long, so unexpected company was a real rarity—and that was how Ken liked it.

"What?" the man demanded as he threw open the heavy wooden door. For a moment it looked as though there was no one there. Then he looked down and saw a little boy, not much more than a metre tall, standing on the porch, shivering in the cold night and staring up at the man with pleading eyes.

"Who are you? What are you doing here?"

"I live here," the tiny waif said.

"You most certainly do not live here. I live here!"

"But I do live here—in the orphanage." The child's voice was as thin as he was.

"Don't be ridiculous, lad. This isn't an orphanage. This is my home. Now away with you, and don't be bothering me again," Ken said firmly.

"I stayed out for a long time, as long as I could. I was scared to come back because I was afraid I'd get into trouble. I just wanted to go for a walk by myself. I went out by the back door without anyone seeing me but I got so cold and lost."

Ken stared at the child. This must be a joke. He knew that there had been a children's home in the area, but that had been many years ago. Orphanages had been a thing of the past for decades. Who did this skinny little brat think he was trying to fool? And what a spot the kid had put him in! He couldn't leave a child out there alone at night. He would have to do something…but what?

"There's not much to you, is there? You'd better not be playing a trick on me, you little urchin," Ken said sternly. "You'd better come in here where it's warmer until we get this sorted out."

The child nodded solemnly and stepped into the house. As he did, his image softened.

"You just stay here in the hall," Ken instructed. "I'm going to call the police. They'll know what to do with you."

There was no answer. Ken turned back toward the little boy and watched in terror as the child's image began to break up and fade away until it was a mere echo of itself, a glistening column of tiny flickering lights that vanished before Ken's eyes.

Grandpa's Goodbye

Stephanie steadied herself against the kitchen counter before answering the phone. She had known the phone call would come, and she had been dreading it. Her husband's tone of voice confirmed that the news was bad.

Rob had stayed in Peterborough to be with his dying father while she had taken their three-year-old daughter to the cottage to protect the child from the inevitable emotional fall-out of her grandfather's death.

Their decision had been a good one. The little girl had spent the week splashing and playing at the beach with Stephanie nearby. This morning, though, a chilly wind had blown in making the lake cold and choppy, so they had stayed indoors.

Rob's voice steadied as he spoke. "Dad went so peacefully. He looked content. He just closed his eyes, really. It was as if he had drifted off to sleep, but at the same time there was something different. I knew he was dead. There was no point in checking his breathing or calling a nurse."

"Oh Rob," Stephanie said quietly. "I'm so sorry. How are you? Do you want me to come into the city to help?"

"I'm okay, hon. We've known for weeks that this was coming. There's just paperwork to do this afternoon, and then tomorrow I'll make the funeral arrangements. It'll be best for me to know that you and Beth are together at the cottage. I'll see you both tomorrow evening."

Stephanie hung up the phone and took a deep breath. Poor Rob. She wished there was something more concrete she could do to help him, but she also knew that his mental image of she and Beth happily at the cottage would help get him through. She pushed herself away from the kitchen counter and turned around to check on Beth.

The child was gone.

"Beth!" the young mother called at the top of her lungs as she checked each room. "Beth, where are you?"

The screen door was open. Stephanie ran outside to the empty yard, screaming her daughter's name. Where did she go? Where to look first? The woods at the side of the cottage—Beth loved it there.

"Beth!… Beth!… Beth!" the frantic woman yelled. The only reply was the wind blowing through the poplars.

What to do? What to do? Where could she be? Stephanie ran frantically, weaving through the trees and calling out her daughter's name as the woods got more and more dense. This wasn't working. What to do? She couldn't search everywhere at once. Panic throbbed through her body. She needed help, but no one would be at the lake until the weekend.

The lake! What if Beth had gone to the beach? The waves were high. There were white caps. Stephanie fled from the woods, tripping on tree roots and underbrush until she was at the clearing in front of the cottage. Panic-stricken, she scanned the beach. There was no sign of the child. Stephanie forced herself to look into the churning water.

"Beth! Beth, don't drown!" she cried out to her empty surroundings before lunging into the cold, hard waves. It was impossible to see to the shallow bottom. Soaking wet and gasping for air, Stephanie knew she had to get back to the cottage and phone for help.

Her body stiff with fright, she willed herself away from the beach. Then the hysterical woman stopped dead in her tracks. Was she hallucinating? She could swear that she saw Beth sitting on the porch steps, smiling happily. *I must be seeing things. She looks as though she's talking to someone.* "Beth! Where have you been? I've been searching all over for you! Are you all right? You know you shouldn't have gone out by yourself!"

"I didn't go out by myself, Mommy. Grandpa came to get me. He took me for a walk. We had fun. I liked it."

"Grandpa came to get you?"

"Yeah! And then he brought me back here to you and he kissed me goodbye."

Don of the Dead

"Josh, come here, quick. Check this out." Michelle called her husband to the front window of their home on a quiet residential street in Hamilton.

"What? That's just old Don Kennedy from down the street, isn't it? He's out for his walk. What's the big deal?"

"It's not a big deal, I guess, except for that big, weird-looking cat trucking along behind him."

"Cat? What cat? There's no cat behind him. For that matter, there's no cat anywhere on the street. Not right now, anyway."

Michelle started to raise her hand to point at the animal trailing behind their elderly neighbour but then stopped herself. For one thing, that was *not* an ordinary cat, and, more importantly, the situation was developing an unnervingly familiar feel to it. If Josh was looking out the same window as she was, and he couldn't see the cat, then in fact she wasn't *seeing* it either. She was *sensing* it.

It had been years since this had happened to her. She'd been in her teens the last time. She'd thought—hoped— that the incidents had stopped. Apparently not. It was definitely best just to let the matter drop. As the young woman turned away from the window, it seemed to her that the cat had angled its head and was staring straight at her. She shuddered and walked to the kitchen to make herself a cup of tea.

A few days later as Michelle was pulling dandelions out of the front lawn, their elderly neighbour walked by again. The two exchanged pleasantries, but as the conversation wound down Don Kennedy asked a question that made Michelle's blood run cold.

"You wouldn't happen to know if the new family that just moved in around the corner has a cat, would you?"

"A cat? Maybe. I don't know," the woman stammered. "Why do you ask?"

The man rubbed his whiskered cheeks before answering. "Well, I don't know, but it's just that every so often these last few days I've been seeing the strangest black cat."

Michelle stood up—too suddenly, she realized immediately, because, just for a second, the world went black at the edges. She took a deep breath and leaned against the fence. "You've seen a strange cat? What's strange about it?"

"Well, I don't know," he began hesitantly. "It's like the thing's wearing a hood."

Michelle babbled something about not having seen anything like that, and how strange it sounded, then said, "You'll have to excuse me, Don. It's time I got in out of the sun."

The young woman made her way toward the house. She was shaky, but she didn't want to go inside. Josh was in there, and right now she needed some time alone. She wouldn't have thought to describe the cat as "wearing a hood," but she could see why her neighbour had. For one thing, the word "cowl" just wasn't in most people's everyday vocabulary. At least now Michelle knew she *had* really seen that cat the other day, though she desperately wished she'd only imagined the thing.

The next day, Michelle and Josh were settling in to enjoy coffee and muffins on their front porch when they heard an odd noise nearby. They hesitated only a moment before hurrying to the sidewalk to investigate.

Josh got there first. "It's Don. He's fallen."

Michelle nodded. "Go call 911. I'll stay with him."

"Don," Michelle said, but she had no idea if the man could hear her or not. She was pretty sure he was still alive, but he certainly wasn't conscious. She wondered if he'd knocked himself out when he'd fallen—or worse— perhaps he'd had a heart attack or a stroke.

He groaned. Relief swept over the young woman. "Oh Don, you *are* alive," she said squeezing his hand. "Just rest. Help is on its way."

Don groaned again, and then Michelle realized that he was trying to speak. "I can't make out what you're saying, Don."

The man's body contorted. His face twisted into a gri- mace. Michelle knelt closer to him. His jaw was twitching with the effort he was exerting just to utter a simple three- letter word. "Cat."

Michelle gasped. Frantically she looked toward her house. Josh was nowhere to be seen. The only other living being nearby was a cat—that same big cat—the black cat with the cowl shrouding its head. The animal turned its head to meet Michelle's gaze. It hissed at her. She shuddered as ice water rippled down her spine. Had the cat hissed?

Or had it cursed at her? *Hurry up, Josh*, she pleaded silently as she cradled her neighbour's head.

Seconds later, Josh came running toward her. "The ambulance is on its way," he yelled. Almost instantly, Michelle could hear an approaching siren.

"You ride with Don in the ambulance," Josh continued as he anxiously knelt down beside his wife. "I'll follow in the car."

Several hours later, Josh drove back home with both Don and Michelle. After several thorough examinations, the doctors determined that Don had just fainted, perhaps because he hadn't taken the time to have breakfast before his walk. Michelle doubted the simplicity of that diagnosis. Thoughts of the black cat crowded everything else out of her mind. Death was riding in the car with them. She could feel it.

After seeing Don safely ensconced in his favourite chair, Josh and Michelle went home. The sight of their muffins covered in flies and their coffee mugs topped with now-curdled milk turned Michelle's stomach. She spent the rest of the day trying, mostly unsuccessfully, to pull herself together and get things ready for going back to work the next day.

In the morning, the woman was still bothered by the events of the day before. *If it hadn't been for that damned cat,* she thought as she passed the bathroom mirror and caught a glimpse of her haggard appearance.

"You have the first shower," she told her husband. "I need to check on Don or I'll just worry about him all day."

When Don didn't answer her knock at his front door, she tried the handle. The door swung open immediately. Michelle was relieved. Obviously the man was awake and had already been at least out on his front porch.

"Hello, Don?" she called, hoping he wasn't in the bathroom. That would be embarrassing for both of them; she wondered if she should just presume he was fine. She could just close the door and go back home to get ready for work. But if she did that, she would worry about him all day. She let herself into the hall and called out for a second time.

Still no answer. She peered into the living room. What a relief! There he was. Poor Don, he must have been tired after all the commotion yesterday because he was still asleep in his recliner, exactly where they'd left him yesterday, though at some point through the night he must have been chilly because he'd covered himself with an old worn black blanket.

Not wanting to startle him, Michelle moved closer to the chair. She screamed. That wasn't any kind of blanket on a sleeping man. That was Don Kennedy's corpse—covered in a layer of black cat fur.

Phantom Mechanic

Every family has its legends, and mine is certainly no exception. Actually, I guess we pretty much have an entire book of them, but the best one by far, the one without which my family would most likely never have existed, is a ghost story—a ghost story and a love story. At least we think it's a ghost story. That's as good a guess as anyone's ever been able to make. We know for sure that it's a love story.

The story begins years ago, in the winter of 1966—long before many of you were born, I'm sure. Certainly before I was born. As a matter of fact, I might not have *been* born if the events in this story had not occurred.

My grandparents, who were not my grandparents at that time but just a young couple in their early twenties, were driving up to North Bay. They'd heard that there were mining jobs there, and a job was something my grandfather, Alan, needed very badly. They already had one child, a son named Scott, and my grandmother, Gwen, was pregnant with my mother. Grandpa Alan had lost his job and, as fond as they were of one another, he and Grandma knew that they couldn't live on love, nor could they risk trying to live on unfounded hopes. They packed up their car and drove off in search of a paycheque.

Like I said, this was the winter of 1966, but the car they were driving was a 1953. A 13-year-old car can be pretty reliable transportation, but apparently, this one was not. It was all they had, though, so they had no choice but to set out in it. On the day they left, by the time they'd said their goodbyes to all their friends and neighbours, it was late afternoon and the sun had set.

Scott, who would grow up to become my uncle, curled himself around his favourite teddy bear in the back seat. My grandmother softly sang him a lullaby. Soon the boy was fast asleep. My grandmother made herself comfortable in the passenger's seat beside Grandpa, and the kilometres rolled by in silence. The same concerns were running through each of my grandparents' minds. Would he be able to find work? And what about accommodation? Who would look after their son when this second child was ready to be born? Grandpa's fingers clenched the cold, hard steering wheel while Grandma stared into the oblivion ahead.

The night was inky black and starless. It had started to snow. The road was narrow, winding and becoming snow-covered. Inside the car, the little boy slept peacefully, wrapped in a cocoon of blankets. His feelings of security might have been inaccurate, but they must also have been all-encompassing, for they allowed his little mind the bliss of unconsciousness.

My grandmother's voice was weak as she asked my grandfather, "Will you be okay driving if I snooze for a bit, dear? I can't stay awake." I've seen lots of pictures of them as a young couple, and the love they had between them was always evident. I never had a problem envisioning that scene.

Grandpa nodded, not daring to look away from the road to meet her loving gaze. The snow was falling more heavily now, almost obscuring his vision. Breaking his concentration by looking away from the road might have been fatal. Although they hadn't seen another vehicle for ages, he had no idea what might be around the next bend.

Not long after, he was actually glad that his wife had fallen asleep. It gave him a feeling of privacy, and he very much wanted to be alone in his increasing nervousness. How had he managed to put his family in jeopardy like this? What foolishness had possessed him to think that he should try to make this drive in this car, and especially at this time of year? Why hadn't he left his wife and child behind until he'd found work? What right did he have to be risking their lives this way?

As his pregnant wife and toddler son slept, my grandfather drove on. Fear chilled him to the core. Driving was becoming a test for both his skills and his emotional control. When the frightened young man steered around the next curve in the road, he was surprised to see lights at the side of the road. It was a service station. Relief poured over him. He pulled onto the lot slowly and gently enough that neither of his sleeping passengers was wakened. Quickly and as quietly as he could, my grandfather stepped out of the car.

"What brings you way out here in this weather?" the service station attendant asked, as the two men approached one another.

The man's innocent and probably well-meaning question was all it took to put my grandfather on the defensive and squelch his plans to ask for help. "Just fill 'er up," he replied, finding that he had to raise his voice to be heard against the gusts of wind cutting through and around the two men.

Setting the nozzle into the opening of the old car's gas tank, the station attendant tugged at the fur-lined hood of his heavy jacket, pulling it until it almost covered his face. "There's a motel about half a mile up the road," the man advised. "You'd be wise to stop and spend the night there. A trucker who came through here an hour ago said the weather was even worse up the highway—a raging blizzard was how he put it. He figured he was just managing to outrun it, but you'll be heading right into it."

Perhaps it was the cockiness of youth, but the man's sensible suggestion put Grandpa even further on the defensive. No one was going to tell him what was best for his family. He was an adult—a man with a wife, a son and another baby on the way. He didn't need anyone's advice. He'd make any decisions that had to be made. Besides, the money they'd have to spend on a room for the night would have to come out of an awfully small stash of cash. They might need that money for food next week once they were safe and sound and settling into their new home.

My grandfather managed to at least be polite and thank the man, who merely shrugged in response. Getting back into the car, Grandpa was pleased to see that his wife and his son were still asleep. As he turned the key in the ignition and steered back out toward the highway, he glanced in the rearview mirror. The snow was coming down so heavily that within seconds he'd lost sight of the man who'd pumped the gas for him, but he knew by the sudden darkness behind him that the man had turned out the lights on his property.

Must be headed for the house I saw behind the station, my grandfather thought as he shifted the car into third gear and eased additional pressure onto the accelerator. Less than five minutes later, he had passed the soft glow of an electric sign at the side of the road—no doubt the motel that the gas station operator spoke of.

The snowfall thickened as he headed along the highway. That nameless trucker that the gas station attendant mentioned was right on the money when he described the storm as a blizzard. Worse, judging from the pinging sound of the white stuff hitting the windshield, it was not just snow that was coming down but ice pellets too. Visibility was virtually zero by now. He was all but driving blind.

In an attempt to see the road ahead, my grandfather adjusted his headlight switch to "high," but it only made things worse. The brighter light made the reflection from the blowing snow even worse, making the visibility even worse. In desperation, he tried the opposite. He turned his headlights off.

It helped! He rejoiced inwardly, but only for a second before realizing that, although he might be able to see a foot or so ahead on the road, no one could see him. Still, the chances of coming across another vehicle were pretty remote. *No one else would be stupid enough to keep driving through this*, he admitted wryly to himself.

As his wife and son slept on, the realization that he alone was responsible for the frozen white hell that his stubbornness had created for all of them tormented him. The soft sounds of their peaceful breathing mocked him. Outside, the staccato pinging of the snow crystals against the car, the gritty slapping of the wipers as they smeared the frozen pebbles across the windshield, the muffled crunching of the tires on snow-covered pavement, and the steady hum of the engine were the only sounds in my grandfather's world.

On he drove, growing more and more terrified each kilometre. He'd long since given up hope that just around a bend, any bend, the weather would clear. He knew now that he was driving right into the worst winter storm he'd ever encountered in his 25 years of life.

Over and over he told himself that the only thing he could do was to keep going, so Grandpa just concentrated on keeping his right foot at a steady angle. Despite this, he was sure they were slowing down. It was also getting colder and colder in the car, and by now it was so cold that his anxious breaths were creating clouds in the air in front of his eyes, reducing his limited visibility even further. He pressed harder on the accelerator, but the car was definitely slowing. Panic rose in his throat. He was sure he could hear his own heart beat. Seconds later the car stopped moving entirely. It had stalled.

Desperately, he twisted the key in the ignition, but he couldn't get it to re-start, and the grinding of the starter motor wakened his wife and son. "There's something wrong with the car. I'm going out to take a look under the hood," he told his wife. "You two go back to sleep."

He watched as my grandmother blew him a kiss before reaching into the back seat and adjusting the covers around her son. His wife's simple gestures made his feelings of guilt worse.

Outside, the gale swirled around Grandpa as he made his way to the front of the car. Feeling under the hood until he found the release latch, he lifted the cover against the wind and stared uncomprehendingly into the engine compartment. Seconds later, a gust of biting snow crystals forced him back into the car. His wife had taken their son from the backseat and had pulled the blankets completely around them both. He knew that they would die—all of them—if he didn't do something to get them out of the freezing storm. *Just a moment longer*, he told himself. *Just let me stay out of that wind a moment longer and then I'll try again to fix whatever's wrong.*

Against his will, the man was beginning to drift off into the frozen oblivion of hypothermia when he felt, more than heard, the hood of his car being raised. For a moment, he actually thought that someone was outside his car. Of course, that was impossible. He was hallucinating or, at the very least, dreaming. Stranger still, his eyes, when he opened them, seemed to confirm what his other senses had told him. The hood of his car was definitely raised.

Concluding that the wind must have sprung the latch, Grandpa groggily stepped out of the car, intending to close the hood. But, there, leaning over into the engine compartment, was a shadowy figure of a man. As my grandfather moved closer to the image, he could hear, through the howling wind, the sound of a screwdriver being worked against metal. The form that had been hunched over the front of the car straightened up and spoke. "Try starting it now," the indistinct presence instructed.

Frightened and confused, my grandfather slipped back into the driver's seat and did as he'd been told. The engine coughed twice before firing to life. With tears of relief and joy coursing down his cheeks, he got back out of the car to thank the skilled Good Samaritan. But the man was gone. In fact, there was nothing, no one, in front of or beside his now-idling car. No person, no vehicle, not even any tire tracks. Stranger still was the sight of a solitary set of footprints in the snow—Grandpa's own.

Bewildered but relieved, he got back into the car, turned it around and drove slowly through the snow in search of the motel he'd passed. It seemed a lifetime ago, but it couldn't have been; only minutes later, my grandfather pulled into the parking lot under the neon sign. He didn't think he'd ever seen a more beautiful sight.

Once they were in their room with little Scott settled in the middle of the sagging double-bed mattress, my grandmother thanked her brave and much-loved husband for managing to fix the car and get them all to safety. My grandfather accepted the praise without argument. It wasn't that he wanted his wife to believe a lie, but that he knew that right now the truth would only upset her.

They made North Bay by noon the next day. On a spring day a few months later, when they were happily established in their new community, my grandfather finally told my grandmother about their lifesaving encounter with the supernatural. As it turned out, the truth brought my grandparents even closer to one another.

Their second child, a daughter who would grow up to become my mother, was born a few weeks later. She and my father were still in their teens when they met and fell in love. I was almost a teenager when Grandpa Alan told me the story of the blizzard that night back in 1966.

I never once got tired of hearing that story. Whenever I visited them in the winter, if the snow and wind were blowing and howling outside, I'd ask Grandpa and Grandma tell me the tale of that dark and stormy night, because no one in my family would exist today if it hadn't been for that very special Good Samaritan—the phantom mechanic.

Nighttime in the Woods

On a perfect summer evening in July 1930, John and Ellen sat side-by-side on the veranda of their Muskoka cottage enjoying the cool night air and the sounds of the animals and birds in the forest beyond their clearing.

"Moving away from the city was the best thing we ever did for ourselves," John said with a contented sigh. "Other than you, the two things I love most in the world are the nighttime and the woods. That makes me a very lucky man. Not too many people can say they have everything they've ever wanted."

Ellen laid her hand on John's and listened as her husband continued to talk. He had a quiet, dignified manner about him that she'd always admired.

"I could never live anywhere else, you know," he said. "I honestly think it would rip my heart out if I had to share this place with anyone but you."

"You're my precious night owl, John." Ellen wanted to say more but didn't dare for fear the worry she was feeling would creep into her voice and give away her dreadful secret. In the 20 years they'd been together, this was the happiest Ellen had ever seen her husband, and that made her heart-wrenchingly sad because she knew something that he didn't.

Ellen had been in town by herself the previous week, shopping for groceries. As she passed the doctor's office on Main Street, the doctor asked her to come inside.

"John was in to see me last week for his regular check-up, and I'm afraid I have some very bad news," he began.

Crushed ice filled the woman's stomach and the room around her began to spin and bob as she listened to the doctor.

He paused to let the woman digest the news as best she could and then cleared his throat self-consciously before going on. "It's a matter of weeks I'm afraid, but he should feel fine almost until his last day, which is why I wanted to talk to you. There's nothing that can be done to help John, so why add worry to his last days if we don't have to?"

"What are you suggesting?" Ellen asked.

"I know this will be hard on you, but I'm wondering if there's any point in telling John that he's going to die."

It took Ellen a minute to react, but when she finally was able to, she nodded in mute agreement with the doctor's suggestion.

Just a few weeks later, Ellen's burden proved to have been worthwhile. John died painlessly in his sleep, blissfully unaware that he'd even been sick. Ellen and the doctor often reflected on their deceitful decision, but neither of them ever had a moment's regret.

It took several years for Ellen to adjust to the reality of John's death, and without the doctor's extraordinary patience and solicitous attentions, she might never have recovered at all. Comfort and companionship had grown from their well-intentioned duplicity during John's final days. Before long their relationship had become the talk of the town. The couple didn't much care about other people's opinions, though. Something much deeper than gossip had forged their bond, and by the time the doctor proposed to Ellen, their union just felt like a natural extension of their friendship.

One evening shortly after the doctor moved to Ellen's isolated home in the woods, the two were sitting comfortably on the veranda after dinner.

"There's something about this place that makes you want to share it with someone you love," Ellen said. "I feel so much happier now than when I lived here alone after John died."

"It's such a peaceful spot, isn't it?" the doctor replied. "The night sounds are soothing. The owl that's hooting sounds as though he's very close by."

Ellen looked up and gasped. An invisible cloak of silence had fallen over the clearing. Just a few metres away, an owl perched on a low branch and stared directly into her eyes. She was sure she'd never seen this particular owl before. She would have recognized it if she had, for a dark stain crusted the feathers on its chest—as if someone had ripped its heart out.

Breaking Up Can Be Deadly

"You can't be serious," Katie was aghast when she saw Jeremy standing on the front porch. He'd ruined her entire summer by breaking up with her in June, right at the end of the school year. Now, just before school was due to start again, there he was at her door. Worse, he looked a total wreck. If he'd hoped to get back in her good books, he could at least have made himself look presentable. His hair was caked with mud, his shirt was ripped and his jeans weren't just dirty, they were filthy.

Anger flooded through Katie's veins. "I hope you're not so stupid as to think I might be interested in getting back together with you."

Jeremy didn't reply. He didn't even move. As a matter of fact, he was still standing mutely, staring at Katie when she slammed the door closed and ran upstairs to her room.

More than an hour later, just as her sobs were easing, Katie's mother called her down for dinner. She knew her eyes were all red and swollen from crying, and she didn't feel up to facing her parents' concerned looks nor her brother's inevitable questions. "I'm not hungry, Mom, and I have a headache. I think I'll just stay up here on my bed if you don't mind."

"Get a cold cloth for your head then and try to have a nap. If you're feeling better later we can go for a stroll," Katie heard her mother say. It seemed odd that her mother wanted to go for a walk, but maybe it would be a good idea. She hadn't bothered to tell her parents when

Jeremy had broken up with her. It was just easier that way. They'd never approved of her relationship with him, and if they'd noticed that he hadn't been around the past two months, they certainly hadn't said anything about it. An evening walk would give Katie a chance to tell her mother everything, including about Jeremy's visit this afternoon.

The young woman slipped quietly into the bathroom, where she splashed cold water on her face until most of the redness and swelling from her crying jag had calmed down. By the time her mother was ready to go, Katie was looking forward to both the walk and the chat. Sault Ste. Marie had been her lifelong home, and she loved this particular neighbourhood best. And today it had another advantage: she was sure she wouldn't see Jeremy because he lived with his parents near the city limits.

"I'm glad you suggested this," Katie told her mother as they reached the end of the block. "It gives us a chance to talk. There's something I've been meaning to tell you."

"Can it wait a few moments, dear? There's something I need to tell you." Her mother's voice sounded odd, strained somehow. It had a brittle edge to it. Katie wondered briefly if there was something wrong with one of her grandparents. "I'm sure you knew that your father and I didn't much like Jeremy or the amount of time you were spending with him last spring. We were actually afraid you'd want to spend every waking moment with him this summer, so I have to tell you we were relieved that he hasn't been around these last couple of months."

"Actually, that's exactly what I wanted to talk to you about," Katie interjected.

"Let me finish, dear," her mother continued. "I was talking to Mrs. Miller this afternoon. Their family had been camping near Chippewa Falls, but they came home early. It seems there's been a terrible tragedy, Katie. Some hikers found Jeremy in the canyon. They found his remains, anyway. As best anyone could tell, he'd fallen and died instantly."

The Light in the Window

When Leanne had paid 10 dollars for the painting at a garage sale in the north end of Oshawa, she'd known that Dennis wouldn't like it. And she'd been right.

"That's the ugliest painting I've ever seen in my life," he'd remarked as she'd awkwardly hefted the oversized frame from the car to the house. "You aren't hoping to hang that thing anywhere in our house, are you?"

"It's not ugly," Leanne had retorted. "It's sophisticated, and yes I am most certainly going to hang it in the house. I have the perfect spot for it in the dining room."

"The dining room? Well, make sure it's not on a wall that I can see from where I sit at the table. I'll choke if I have to look at that while I'm eating. The thing's appalling. I mean, what is it? It's a solid black background with a big black silhouette of a house. There's nothing even interesting about that. Who wants an all black painting?"

Leanne sighed. "Obviously I do, and anyway, it's not all black. It's a nighttime scene and you're right, the house is a silhouette, but see up there in the corner? There's a tiny light shining through the attic window. That's the part of the picture I like the best."

Several months later, Dennis still occasionally grumbled about Leanne's taste in artwork, but for the most part the issue had been dropped and their lives had gone on. They were even planning a dinner party.

"We'll keep it small so that it's intimate," Leanne suggested. Dennis rolled his eyes.

"If we just invite two other couples we can serve the meal formally, in the dining room."

"Yeah okay, but don't change my place at the table. If you do, you'd better take the painting down. Where I sit now is the only chair in the room where you can't see that black beast."

Leanne nodded. She had no intention of taking down the painting or changing Dennis' seat at the dinning room table, but she had every intention of hosting a nice get-together.

Predictably, the dinner guests all commented on the painting. It *was* eye-catching, which was one of the reasons Leanne had been attracted to it in the first place. When her girlfriend's husband commented that the picture was all black, she jumped to the artist's defence.

"But it isn't! If you look carefully at the dark house you'll see that there's a light shining through the attic window," Leanne said as she walked toward the painting with her arm extended, ready to point out her favourite feature of the piece.

But the light wasn't shining. There was no light any-where in the painting. It was all black.

Leanne's temper did a slow burn all through dinner. Dennis must have painted over the yellowy glow in the window of the house. He'd occasionally played practical jokes on her, but this wasn't even a little bit funny. This was vandalism, and when their company left that evening she told him so in no uncertain terms. Of course he pleaded complete innocence, but how else could it have happened?

They stared at one another as the atmosphere between them chilled to frosty. It was clear they were giving one another the silent treatment. Neither one was about to give an inch, to the point that when the phone rang just before bedtime they both ignored it. It wasn't until 7:30 the next morning when Leanne cleared the phone's answering machine that they learned one of their guests from dinner the previous night had suffered a fatal heart attack while driving home.

It took fully a month for Dennis and Leanne's life to return to normal. During the mental and emotional turmoil of coming to grips with their friend's death, they each promised to themselves to treat the other with more respect and kindness. Which is why when Leanne noticed that the light in the painting was once again shining through the attic window like a beacon of hope, she was touched by Dennis's gesture of repair. Oddly, when she tried to thank him for touching up the tiny spot on the painting, he denied doing it as vehemently as he had when she had accused him of painting over it. After that, neither one of them mentioned the painting again.

By the end of summer, they were both feeling that the wound of their friend's death had healed a bit and that it would be good to invite some people over for a meal.

"Let's make this a family thing," Leanne suggested. "How about just your parents and mine?"

"We're not serving any booze, then—not even wine," Dennis said firmly. "You know my father. Once he gets started he just doesn't stop until he gets totally obnoxious."

Leanne agreed immediately. Dennis's mother was a fine woman, but his father, well…he was fine too, unless he was drinking. Alcohol would get the best of that man eventually, she was sure.

The night of the family dinner, Leanne set the table carefully. She put out her good wine glasses in anticipation of serving a sparkling cider that she'd found. *This is going to be a good evening*, she thought as she stood back and glanced over the room.

The painting! The painting was all black again. There was no light shining through the attic window. How could Dennis do something like that? He must have known it would upset her. Honestly, his sense of humour could be so tasteless.

Leanne stormed into the kitchen ready to lace into her husband, but he was talking on the telephone and clearly the conversation was not going well. He hung up, turned to her and said, "It's my father. He went to the liquor store to buy some wine to bring to the party tonight. Someone ran a red light. Dad's dead."

In the dark, early hours of the next day, when Dennis had finally fallen asleep, Leanne tiptoed downstairs to the dining room. The tiny light shone through the attic window in the painting once again. She lifted the frame off the wall and carried it outside to the garbage.

The next time she went out, the painting was gone.

The Cabin in the Woods

Jeff gunned the snowmobile's engine, grinning with the joy of hearing it roar. He'd waited for years to get to this mammoth system of trails around Kapuskasing and now, finally, he was here. He felt like a kid in a toy store. He had his brand new, high-end machine and kilometres upon kilometres of pristine snow.

Steering the powerful sled through the deep powder and up an incline, Jeff yelled in delight as a blanket of white covered him completely and obscured his helmet's visor. Adrenaline surged through his veins. He leaned to correct the machine's angle—didn't need vision to do that. Jeff had always ridden by the seat of his pants, by touch, by feel. That sensation was a huge part of what made snowmobiling so darned much fun. Every ride needed at least one good white-out. They weren't often this fantastic, though; he was totally engulfed in snow for longer than he'd ever been. This would be a story and a half to tell at the clubhouse. Wow, what a ride!

When the blizzard of snow swirling around him settled a bit, Jeff was disappointed. He always wished the rush could last forever, and that one had been the most spectacular moment he'd ever had on a machine. It had been so strong that it had left him with a headache.

This getaway had been everything he had hoped for—well worth the years of waiting. The possibility of quitting his job, pulling up stakes and moving to the north flashed across his mind. He could spend next summer sorting out the practicalities of that plan, but it would be amazing to live close by wilderness like this and be ready to enjoy the first good dump of snow next season.

Jeff coasted to the crest of a gentle incline. The blowing snow had misted the inside of his visor. He eased to a stop and took off his helmet.

Would you look at that? Unbelievable! There before his eyes stood a pristine, 30-year-old snowmobile! Someone must have ridden it to the small log cabin nestled in the woods a short distance away from the trail. Jeff could hardly wait to talk to whoever owned that old sweetheart of a snow machine, and he could do with a drink of water to ease the discomfort of his pounding headache. Mostly though, he wanted to look more closely at that old snow machine. It was an exact duplicate of the picture he had cut out of a catalogue and pinned up on his bedroom wall when he was a kid. Those were the days when just riding a friend's toboggan or snow saucer down a hill was a big deal.

He hurried to the cabin door, mildly surprised that he was walking quickly, not with the usual waddle of someone wearing a snowmobile suite. The pine-board door was ajar. Jeff gave a cursory knock with his mittened knuckles and called in a hello.

"Hello yourself," a man with a badly out-of-style moustache replied as he limped to the door. "I'm glad you're here. It's time for me to move on."

Confused, Jeff watched the man get on the old snowmobile. "Wait, man, you can't ride like that in just a shirt and pants. Don't be ridiculous. You'll freeze to death."

"I'm fine, son. The cabin is all yours now," he called before a sudden gust of wind blew toward the cabin door, swirling up a curtain of snow and blocking Jeff's vision. When the snowflakes cleared, the man was nowhere in sight—not even any tracks. The blowing snow must have covered them over.

Shaking his head, Jeff hesitantly stepped inside. Wow! He could hardly believe his eyes. It was obvious that someone had gone to a lot of trouble to set up this room, but a long time ago—30 years ago or more—which was a bit of a coincidence because that was the vintage of the machine parked outside.

Jeff stomped the snow off his boots and walked farther into the room, calling out hello only to ease his own sense of being an intruder. As he looked around, taking in his surroundings, his feelings of intruding vaporized. This wasn't that stranger's cabin. This was a place that Jeff knew well. This was his bedroom—the one he'd had at home when he was a kid.

Look, there was his desk in the corner where it always had been, littered with books and magazines, mostly about snowmobiles. He had spent hours scanning through those magazines, studying the pictures and reading the articles over and over again. He smiled. His mother had been right. His room was a mess, but it was his mess, his very own magical mess, and he'd always loved spending time in here.

Even his model airplanes were here, strung from tacks pushed into the ceiling. He'd been proud of building those planes. The detail on each one still amazed him. And that poster over his bed! It had come in a special edition catalogue of snow machines. The one pictured was identical to the one that man had ridden off on, leaving him alone here.

Wait. What was he thinking? This was a cabin in the wood near Kapuskasing. It wasn't his childhood bedroom in Kingston. A wave of nausea and dizziness washed over him. Jeff peered out the door. There was already a light dusting of snow on his snowmobile.

Then he looked back into the cabin—the cabin that was somehow his old bedroom. He sighed and laid his lifeless body on his old, familiar bed while his soul prepared for the ride of a lifetime.

The Salesman

Mel was a salesman—a born salesman—and it's no wonder. The sales game was in his genes. His father had been the best there was, and while Mel might not have been as good as the old man, he was good—really, really good. Always had been.

In the 1980s, for instance, Mel had ridden the crest of the waterbed craze; then just as people were getting fed up with sloshing around while they were sleeping, he had jumped into the emerging cell-phone market. That was back when the things were the size (and weight!) of a brick, and the demand for cell phones had only gotten bigger since then.

The trouble was, Mel was never quite as moral a man as his father had been. Not that he ever did anything outright illegal, but he was awfully good at cutting corners—a little too good at it—and by the dying days of the 20th century, Mel's manoeuvres had caught up to him. The big marketers wouldn't hire him, and even the smaller, almost fly-by-night outfits, were wary. As a result, Mel was getting up close and personal with destitution.

One autumn afternoon as he sat in the old, overstuffed chair that had come with the furnished room he rented near McLeod and Bank streets in Ottawa, Mel was half-heartedly wondering how he would pay the next week's rent when he came across an interesting little filler piece in the city's local rag:

Kanata Family Flees Haunted House
A family fled from their home in the middle of the night yesterday, saying that the house was haunted. Just after midnight the couple, Bruce and Jodie Williamson, hurriedly gathered their two children and made a run for their mini-van. They spent the night in a nearby motel.

Bruce Williamson reported that the trouble started soon after his wife purchased a hall table from an estate sale. Williamson is now convinced that a spectre came into his house with the piece of furniture.

Initial signs of the haunting were subtle, and the couple didn't suspect that the unexplained annoyances were actually paranormal activity. Jodie Williamson explained that when they left small personal articles such as gloves and car keys on the newly purchased table, the items would often be on the floor just moments later.

"It was aggravating for sure, but mostly we tried to ignore it. A few days later, though, both the dishwasher and the kitchen radio started turning on when no one was near them, and Bruce's electric razor sparked out in his hand when he turned it on. Plus we just sensed a presence. It sounds crazy because we couldn't see anyone, but it really felt as though there was another person in the house."

Bruce added that when his daughter claimed to have heard her favourite teddy bear growl, he at the time chalked it up to a child's over-active imagination. Now he's not so sure.

"Last night when I was washing my face before bed, I heard a strange buzzing sound coming from the ceiling. I looked up, and that's when I saw them—flies, a thick swarm of flies—thousands of them, honestly—up in the skylight. Man, I was totally freaked out."

Understandably, the Williamsons left the house immediately after that with little more than the clothes they were wearing.

Authorities are looking into the matter.

A small smile crept across Mel's face before blossoming into a full-blown grin. Sheer delight surged through his veins. He pumped his fist in the air and shouted, "Yes!" to the empty room. For the first time, he was glad to be in the situation that he was in; if it hadn't been for the downhill slide in his sales career, he wouldn't have spent the past three months holed up watching television 15 hours a day, and if he hadn't watched all those cheesy reality horror shows, he would never have had this revelation.

Mel said a silent blessing to the producers of every one of those ghostbuster shows where dudes with supposedly psychic powers go to haunted places and get rid of whatever spirit was supposed to be haunting the place. Every show was always so completely over-the-top bogus that Mel knew he would have no trouble stepping into the role and selling himself as a ghostbuster.

The location of this particular haunting made it a bit of a challenge for a man who hadn't owned a car in five years. Taking the bus would take too long, and besides, it wouldn't give the right impression. He could rent a car. Yes, that's exactly what he would do—he would rent a car—a luxury car to boot. Let them presume that he was so good at getting rid of spooks that he had already made a bundle at it.

Clothes were another problem; he really didn't have anything decent to wear. All of his clothes were not only out of style but also downright shabby, but he didn't want to buy new ones just yet because if his initiation into the field of spiritual cleansing didn't go well, he could find himself in the middle of next week with newly purchased clothes and no money for food. He would just have to affect rumpled disinterest in fashion. At least that part of the scheme would be honest.

Devising the exorcism routine was the least of Mel's worries. The sales game was all about creativity and showmanship, and Mel had those qualities in spades. He soaked the label off an empty eye-drop bottle and poured a few drops of out-dated vegetable oil into it. His secret potion was ready to go. By the time he walked out the door of the old rooming house, Mel's step was lighter than it had been for years. This was going to be a licence to print money.

Three hours later, he was back at home one hundred dollars richer, having returned the rental car after making an enormous show of rubbing cooking oil on the underside of the Williamsons' table.

What a gig! Why hadn't he thought of this before? He had even given the family some advice, telling them that for the next three months they weren't to dust the bottom of the table, that they were to be extremely careful how they placed small objects such as keys on the table, and that an orderly house was not just a tidy house but a spiritually clean house. And then, just because he felt like having fun, he explained that once a day for 10 minutes, they should stand by the table, holding hands and willing the spirit to go free and be at peace.

By the time Mel left the Williamson house, he knew he had his groove back.

Early the next morning his landlady knocked on Mel's door. "Some people here to speak to you," she told him, nodding toward the building's small foyer.

A bill collector? The police? No, he'd been keeping a low profile. Obviously he must have attracted someone's attention somehow. "Tell them I'll be right there," Mel said.

After tucking in his shirt and combing his hair, Mel plastered on his salesman smile and made his way to the foyer, where a haggard-looking couple sat waiting for him.

"You have to help," the woman implored.

Mel stared at the pair, confused.

"The Williamsons' neighbours are friends with my sister-in-law. We heard that you got rid of the ghost that haunted their table. Our haunting is way worse than theirs. Please help us. We'll pay you anything you ask."

Mel stroked his chin, partly to stall for time and partly to be sure he didn't start to chuckle. This ghostbusting was going to be a far better gig than he had ever imagined. Thinking fast, he said, "If I go with you right now there'll be an additional emergency call-out fee on top of my regular charges, but if you're willing to pay that, I'll come right along with you now and take care of the problem."

"Oh please, yes, money is no object," the woman assured him. "We can't live with this any longer. She's transparent but we can see her perfectly clearly, even make out the details of her clothing. She's wearing an old-fashioned maid's uniform, and it's obvious from the way she glances around that she's really anxious about something. It's awful to watch, I can assure you."

Mel nodded and took a deep breath. He went back to his room and grabbed his bottle of cooking oil, and less than five minutes after first setting eyes on them, Mel was in the backseat of the couple's car. He informed them that he needed complete silence until they reached the haunted house. The couple assured him that they understood completely. He doubted that they understood at all that what he needed was to concentrate on working up a routine for the supposed exorcism.

In the end, he did much the same routine as he had done in the Williamson home, only this time he sprinkled a few drops of cooking oil in the corners of each room in the house. His instructions as he left in a taxi were essentially the same ones he had left with the Williamsons: they were to hold hands and meditate in every room for 10 minutes every day.

Two hours later, Mel was back in his room counting out five hundred dollars. He had hit the sweet spot—an untapped niche market. Mel, the cracker-jack salesman, was undeniably back on top.

And he stayed there too—for about three days. That was when it started. Every few minutes the table by the door would lift up at an angle and tap out a rhythm on the floor, and then an image of a woman wearing a white bonnet and an apron over a black dress would float across his room, just slightly above floor level.

Mel was facing the toughest sales job of his career: selling himself on the theory that his small room wasn't haunted. It was one deal he couldn't close. The next day he left the rooming house forever. He owed rent, but even so the landlady was glad to see the back of him. He had begun acting really oddly. She'd had that type through her place before, and she knew he would only get stranger and stranger.

These days Mel is often seen shuffling along Elgin Street, muttering to himself and flailing his arms as though he's batting at insects buzzing around his head. Every now and again he glances furtively over his shoulder, looking for the invisible presence that never leaves his side. He tries to sell himself on the theory that the ghost is just a figment of his addled brain. Somehow it's less frightening for him to think he's insane than to accept the reality that he is haunted and will be to his dying day.

Reunion

"It's so great that everyone could make it to Grand Valley this year. This land Grandma and Grandpa bought is such a beautiful spot. It's perfect for these reunions." Debbie paused and surveyed her family's faces. All but one person around the campfire knew that one of the best parts of their annual gathering was about to unfold. "Now that night has fallen and the campfire is burning, it's time to roast some marshmallows and choose people to tell ghost stories. Do we have any volunteers to be this year's first storyteller?"

Joe's hand shot up.

"You're going to start, Joe?" Surprise was evident in Debbie's voice.

"No, not me. I was going to volunteer Ashley. I think she should take the first turn. After all, she's new to the family, seeing as she and I have just gotten together and all." A ripple of agreement ran through the crowd. "And that way too, we're sure to get a fresh story, one that none of us has ever heard before."

The young woman sitting beside Joe gave him an exaggerated dirty look as twenty-some other people began clapping and chanting and calling out for Ashley to entertain them. Good naturedly, she stood up. "I wish someone had let me know that story-telling was to be part of your family's reunion," she said. "I might have come prepared."

"Yeah, or you might not have come at all," Joe's younger brother, Greg, teased.

Ashley nodded. "You're right. I might have considered staying home, especially considering I don't know any ghost stories."

"Then you'd better make one up quick," another voice called out.

"Well okay, it looks as though I'm not going to be able to weasel my way out of this, so I'll give it a go. The only story I can think to tell you isn't really a ghost story, but I always thought it was pretty scary, so maybe it'll be a good enough substitute."

"Sounds good," Debbie confirmed.

"Well, as far as I know this is a true story; I'm not making it up, anyway, that's for sure. This is a tale my great aunt used to tell my sister and I when we were kids. See my aunt and her brothers and sisters were raised just west of here, when the place was just farms and countryside—not all full of houses like it is now—and what I'm going to tell you about happened when her parents were kids, so in other words, a very long time ago."

A hush fell over Ashley's audience. She'd captured everyone's attention, that was clear.

"It seems a boy named Oliver lived with his family near my great aunt's family farm. Every morning after he'd done his chores, Oliver would go out to play in the woods. His parents didn't mind because he was always home by lunchtime, and really there was nothing anywhere around that could harm him—or at least that's what his parents thought. One day, Oliver didn't come home for lunch. Needless to say, his parents were worried, and they hurried outside to look for him."

Ashley's description had effectively taken her listeners right back in time to that old farm kitchen. Each person around the campfire could imagine the anxiety that Oliver's parents must have been feeling and could picture them frantically rushing into the woods to search for their child.

"An icy, howling wind had blown up and was swirling through the woods. Oliver's father called out to the boy. 'Son, can you hear me? Where are you? It's your father.'

"'Oliver! Oliver!' his mother repeated.

"But there was no answer. It seemed to the parents as though their child had vanished, without a trace. Sobbing, the couple kept searching and calling for their son.

Finally, off in the distance, they heard a familiar voice. It was Oliver calling to them.

"'Where are you, lad?' the father shouted.

"'I'm here, Father. Can you see me?'

"The angry, noisy wind picked up strength.

"'No Ollie, we can't see you. Tell us where you are, Oliver,' his mother pleaded.

"'I don't know, Mother. I don't know where I am.'

"As the child spoke his voice became fainter and fainter, as if the wind was stealing it away. Finally his heartbroken parents couldn't hear him at all."

Ashley paused. The people around the campfire barely dared to breathe. They were all desperate to know the conclusion to the strange tale. When it appeared that she wasn't going to say anything else, Greg called out, "But what's the rest of the story? Where *was* Oliver? Was he hiding? Did they find him? Did they get him back?"

Still standing, Ashley shook her head. "I can't really tell you the rest of the story because there isn't one. To this day no one knows what became of Oliver. He was never seen again."

"That's a sad story," Debbie said quietly.

Ashley nodded. "My great aunt would always cry when she told it. What made it worse for her was that every now and again, when the wind blew across the fields in a certain way, she swore that way off in the distance she could hear a child's voice calling for help."

A heavy cloak of silence hung over the group sitting by the fire. No one knew what to say. Finally someone said,

"Well Joe, thanks for bringing Ashley to our family. We need good storytellers, and she's certainly that."

A twitter of nervous laughter ran through the circle of relatives, and then silence returned. Perhaps they were listening to hear Oliver's cry for help.

The Times, They Are Changing

"Hurry, Matt. You'll be sorry if you miss the last roller coaster run of the season," Joanne called over her shoulder. "It's your last chance till next year."

Matt's friend had no idea how very wrong she was. He wasn't going to be sorry at all. Not after that summer in high school when he'd worked the carnival circuit and had seen up close and personal just exactly how drugged-out and hungover some of those roadies were when they put those rides together. Ever since then, he'd always avoided any opportunity to plunk his sorry butt onto the cold metal seat of any ride at any fairground.

Like everyone else his age, he'd come to Grand Bend for the surfing, and he had easily fallen in with a terrific group of friends. They had bonded pretty much instantly by challenging and supporting one another on the waves, and Matt certainly didn't want to risk losing their respect by having them find out he was deathly afraid of amusement park rides. "You guys go ahead. I'll catch up," he answered, pointing to a line of portable toilets.

As Matt watched his friends disappear around a turn in the midway, he smiled, satisfied that he had successfully managed to avoid the terrifying experience of hurtling out of control in rickety machinery while at the same time saving face. He was impressed with himself and very content just to wander past the booths where hucksters urged him toward their game, whatever it might be, for the sole purpose of separating him from his money. There was such a sameness to the all those dudes—not just their patter but even their looks. Matt supposed it was only logical; they were all essentially pushing the same con, which was part of the reason that the young woman standing outside a small black tent caught his eye.

As soon as he realized he'd been staring at her, Matt nodded and mumbled something that sounded a bit like "hello" just so as not to seem rude.

"And to you too," she replied, holding his gaze.

Matt looked around uncomfortably. What to do? Walk away or start a conversation?

"My friend, you need your fortune told." She held the tent flap aside for him. "Come in."

The air inside the tent was damp and still and thick with a bitter scent that smelled like wet cardboard.

"Spill a bottle of patchouli in here?" Matt asked, hoping to sound slightly derisive. The smell was making him a bit dizzy. He leaned against a table. His stomach heaved.

"Sit," the woman ordered. She ran the bony fingers of her right hand down his arm.

It was odd how quiet the tent was. Why couldn't he hear the noise from the midway? His head spun.

He looked up at the woman. How could he have thought she was young? She was ancient, maybe the oldest person he'd ever seen.

"I am Sophia," she whispered and then waited for Matt to introduce himself. When he didn't she shrugged and expelled a cloud of foul breath. "No matter. Your name is not important, but my message to you is. You will make a fatal error in judgment tonight—at exactly 1:30 AM."

Matt bolted up from the chair. Where was the door to this stupid tent? He had to get out. *Gonna hurl. Or faint. Or both. Can't breathe.* He tripped on the tent pole and stumbled, falling to the ground face first, but at least he was back outside. He gasped for air. His chest heaved and his hands shook. He could hear rhythmic chanting sounds coming from the dank depth of the tent.

Just slow down man, slow down. Nothing happened. Get a grip. His breathing calmed. In the distance he could hear someone calling him. Was the old crone coming after him? *Get a life, dork. That's Joanne calling. There she is.*

"You're a big goof. You missed the best few minutes of your life, Matt. It was great."

Matt shook his head and struggled to get a breath. When he dared to speak, his words tumbled out in a frenzy. "Let's get a drink."

"Yeah, for sure, but don't you want to wait for the others?" Joanne's tone made it more than obvious that she was waiting for him to explain himself. It wasn't like Matt to be in a rush to do anything except get to the beach. She took his arm. His muscles were taut. It was clear he wasn't in a mood to talk. The darkening sky concealed

Matt's features, but still she could see that he looked stressed. "What's up?"

Matt replied by shaking his head. He was nowhere near ready to explain what had just happened to him.

They got to the pub ahead of the others. Matt ordered two shooters.

"I don't want a drink, thanks Matt," Joanne told him, presuming the second one was for her.

"I do," he replied, draining the nearest shot glass.

What the hell kind of a weird thing had just happened to him? '*A fatal error in judgment*,' *she said. What the hell? Who does that old lady think she is, anyway?* Too much—it was too much. His hands shook as he let the liquid from the first shot glass burn his throat. He wiped the dribble from the side of his lip with one hand as he picked up the second glass with his other hand.

"Matt?" Joanne whispered. "What's wrong?"

"Nothing. I need to get drunk, that's all."

"What the heck happened back there?"

Matt ignored her question and ordered another drink. The cool liquid burned his throat a little less each time he drained a glass until finally, fleetingly, the world lost its edges and the old-woman fortune teller was gone. She had never existed. Then she hurtled herself back into Matt's consciousness and swirled around there before leaching into his body.

Suddenly his friends were pressing their faces close to him—too close. He moved his head to the side. They were all leaning over him, their faces pulsing first closer and then farther away. He closed his eyes and welcomed utter blackness.

When he came to again, he was on the floor of a small room—it looked like a hotel room. The bed was unmade. Someone must have taken him here and put him to bed. How humiliating. Worse, he'd obviously fallen out of bed like a little kid. The whole thing was childish, really. He wouldn't ride the roller coaster because he was chicken—everyone from grade one on had known Matt was a wimp. Then he gets drunk like a rookie teenager and gets put to bed like a baby.

He propped himself up on his elbow. The room spun madly around his head, but he managed to spot a clock on the nightstand. Hah—it was 2:15 AM. He hadn't died at 1:30 like that stupid gypsy had told him he would. He pulled himself up onto the bed and with a great force of will gathered his clothes around him. Only a loser wakes up in some hotel room. He would get home tonight if it killed him. He splashed water on his face, opened the door and staggered down the corridor toward the exit sign. Seconds later he was in his car.

It took forever to get the key into the ignition. Cursing his shaking hands, he aimed the small piece of metal time and time again until finally he felt the key slide into the slot. The radio came on—too loud—but anything was too loud right now.

He whimpered from the exertion of trying to keep his world in focus. He wrestled the gearshift lever into drive and noticed the small numbers on the dashboard clock; 2:25 AM and he was still alive.

"Stupid old bag!" he screamed into the empty car. He pressed his foot down on the accelerator pedal—at least he thought he did. *Press harder, you dumb dork.*

When they found his body twisted into his mangled car, the radio was still playing.

"Don't forget folks, tonight's the night we go back to standard time. If you didn't fix them at 2:00 AM then now's the time to turn your clocks back an hour."

Eliza's Marker

There's probably not a soul on this earth who doesn't have some sort of a reaction when he or she walks through a graveyard. Some people might worry about disturbing the souls of those buried beneath the soil, while others might be forced to contemplate the reality of their own mortality. Despite any thoughts or fears we're obliged to acknowledge when we're near those who have been laid to rest, graveyards themselves are generally pretty peaceful places.

But not all bodies are laid to rest so formally. The pioneers of this province often had to make do with much less official space, and farmyard burials were often a necessity. Even so, the mourners would try to mark the plots respectfully with a dignified marker commemorating their loved one. There's one plot on a tract of old farmland roughly halfway between Owen Sound and Walkerton, however, that is guaranteed to give anyone a scare they'll never forget.

A couple named Eliza and Ernie owned that land well over 150 years ago. Eliza was said to have been the kindest woman ever to have walked the earth. Ernie was nothing short of a miserable cuss. Everyone wondered how she could put up with him, but perhaps it was simply that, given the time and place, she had no choice.

One lovely morning in the summer of 1875, a neighbour went to call on Eliza. The door to the farmhouse stood open, so when no one answered her knock, the neighbour went in. There on the floor lay Eliza's lifeless body. She had been strangled. Ernie was nowhere to be found.

The people from farms from kilometres around were devastated by the news of Eliza's death. There hadn't been a murder in these parts for as long as anyone could recall. They formed a posse and searched for Ernie, but he was long gone. So they did the only thing they could do. They held a small funeral for the deceased and buried her remains in the soil just outside her home. Then the local carpenter carved out Eliza's name, along with some kind words about her, on a slab of lumber and propped the makeshift monument up at the head of the grave.

A few weeks later, a handful of neighbours met at Eliza and Ernie's old house. They planned to spruce the place up a bit in the hopes that another couple might move to the area and take over the farm. It was a good solid house, and the land was fertile.

But no one ever lived on that land again. A strange phenomenon had begun to appear on Eliza's grave marker.

At first there only seemed to be an oddity in the wooden marker, but soon it was obvious: an outline of a face was forming just above her name. Over the next few weeks that outline became so clear that Ernie's face was readily recognizable. It was as if Eliza was telling everyone, in the only way she could, who had murdered her.

Chapter 3: Full Moon

Twin Terror

Dianne sat bolt upright in bed. Rivers of cold sweat traced every crevice and crease on her body. Gasping for air, she willed herself to open her eyes and scan the darkened bedroom. "You're such a wimp," she whispered to herself with considerable relief.

She walked to the window and looked out. The full moon cast a protective light over the town of Sutton. Content in the knowledge that whatever had wakened her had only been a dream, the young woman lay back down and pulled the covers up over her shoulders. As she waited for her heart rate to ease, she wondered what it was she'd been dreaming of.

A fragment of an ephemeral memory surfaced—a dark, enclosed space. Was there a face? Yes, there was a face— a somehow-familiar face. Then the image vaporized too quickly for her conscious mind to grasp. Frustrating. But the dream-induced amnesia might just be the blessing that would let her get back to sleep...

Twenty minutes later, Dianne jolted upright again. The sound of her own screaming had wakened her. She was tangled in the sheets and on the edge of the bed. This timeshe remembered. She'd been dreaming about a man chasing her.

It was the strangest scene; she could see herself as clear as could be. It was like she wasn't part of the dream but was watching it. He had caught her. He had been carrying something. He had hit her with it, over and over again. The dream had been so real that even now, fully awake, she gingerly ran her hands over her head and body to make sure she was all right.

What would have made her dream such an awful thing? That man, who was he? There was something familiar about him, very familiar, but she couldn't quite place him. And where was she in the dream? It was somewhere dark, but where?

Dianne hadn't had a nightmare this bad since she was a kid. She needed to get up and walk around to shake this one off. Splash some water on her face, maybe make a cup of hot chocolate and bring it back to bed. It was just before 3:00. She'd need to get some more sleep or she'd never make it through her day at work.

Determined to forget the senseless nightmare, Dianne stood beside her bed. For a moment, it seemed as though her legs weren't going to hold her. And she remembered something else; in her dream, she'd been wearing a blouse that wasn't hers. It belonged to Donna, her twin sister. Dianne had never thought the colour was flattering. Why would she dream she was wearing it? "Sheesh girl, everything about that dream has you freaked," she told herself before taking an initial step away from the bed.

A second later, a series of electronic tones made her scream for the second time that night. She looked around wildly, trying to place the sound and finally realizing it was just her cell phone. Dianne grabbed the phone and squinted at the caller ID on the tiny illuminated screen. Donna? Why would her twin sister be calling in the middle of the night?

"Donna, what's wrong? Is everything okay?"

"Help! Ted's trying to kill me! He has a bat! I'm hurt. Come—"

The last thing Dianne heard before the line went dead was her sister's blood-curdling scream.

Playing with Time

"You can't be serious? We can go shopping any time we want when we're back at home, but this is the only afternoon we'll be able sit here by the Avon River." Lynne looked along the park bench at her sister.

"If you knew anything at all about antiques and collectibles, you would know that Stratford is famous for its unique little shops," Lesley replied.

"Knock yourself out then. I'll enjoy the fresh air and sunlight while you're in a bunch of dusty hole-in-the-wall stores inhaling potpourri," Lynne said, shrugging her shoulders dismissively.

It was unusual for her not to agree with her older sister's plans, but today she was just too relaxed and content to be bothered putting any energy into the sibling balancing act. They had tickets to see Shakespeare's *Macbeth* that evening, but for now she just wanted to enjoy the ambience by the river and watch the swans with their cygnets glide across the water.

Lynne offered a wave goodbye and let the sun's warmth soak into her body. She closed her eyes, took a few deep breaths and was drifting into a daydream when someone sat down at the other end of the bench. She looked up to find a man sitting next to her. Too surprised to be subtle, she jerked her body away from his.

"Sorry, I don't mean any harm," the man said. "I just needed to get out of that stuffy tent and away from work for a while."

Lynne stared at him. There were empty benches and tables scattered about the park. Why did he sit right next to her? Was he some kind of a weirdo? Was he dangerous? Should she run? He just looked like a middle-aged man— nothing extraordinary. Where would she run to, anyway, especially as Lesley might come back… *Hey, this dude's chatting away to me, like we're having a conversation or something. He's gotta be a nutcase*, she thought as the man lifted his arms in an exaggerated motion and declared, "I'm sure you'll agree that I just didn't have any choice."

Lynne squirmed. She nodded mutely as though she'd heard and understood and agreed with everything the man had told her.

"It is terribly ungentlemanly of me to have intruded on your privacy the way I have, but I must say I feel so very much better for our little chat, and I do thank you for your kindness to an old fuddy-duddy like me. The way I'm carrying on, you would think I was new to the theatre, but as I said, my responsibilities are particularly onerous with this production, and I've so appreciated being able to get the tiresome details off my chest by talking things over with you."

His words tumbled out one after another with clipped precision, as though he'd been trained to speak clearly.

There was something intriguing and just a bit familiar about him. *Either the sunshine is affecting my brain, or that man is an actor. Lesley will never believe this.*

The man stood up and reached into his jacket pocket. A gun? Lynne jumped. *Maybe he's not an actor; maybe he's dangerous.*

"Here, let me thank you for your kind patience by giving you this copy of the program from opening night. I've signed it, of course." The man thrust a booklet in Lynne's hand. It felt as though she was holding a sheet of ice. She looked down. He'd given her an old-fashioned theatre program. The pages were yellowed and brittle. She looked up to thank the man, but he was gone.

For a moment she sat alone, blinking into the bright sunlight. Maybe she should have gone with Lesley. Then it struck her why the man looked familiar. He was Donald Morrow, the actor from that old television series that she and Lesley had loved when they were teenagers.

A moment later her sister was beside her again, excitedly describing the fun she'd had on the local main street. "You should've come with me. You wouldn't believe what an interesting time I've had. I hope you weren't bored."

"Bored? Hardly. I'm positive that I met the actor from *The Conquerors*, that old TV show. Remember? I met the guy who played the detective; I'm positive."

"Nice try, Lynne. He died about 10 years ago."

Lynne tucked the theatre program under her purse and out of sight. It wasn't cold any longer, but it had started to crumble. The top right corner had just fallen off.

Lesley tugged at her arm. "Come on! Are you going to sit there all day? Let's go get some dinner. I'm famished, and I saw the cutest little diner not far from…"

Lynne let her sister ramble on. Gently she lifted her purse from the bench beside her. There was the program—proof positive that she had met Donald Morrow. She remembered now; he'd started his career as a Shakespearean stage actor. He must still love it or he wouldn't be at Stratford again this year. He certainly couldn't need the money.

Lesley bent to pick up the souvenir he'd left for her. And as she did, the autographed program crumbled into tiny particles of dust and dissolved into the air.

The Haunted Ghost Walk

Andy wiped hamburger grease from his fingers as his brother Dave stood up and pointed at the clock above the counter at the fast food restaurant. Customers sitting at nearby tables stared as the pair wrapped long, black cloaks around their shoulders and picked up their lanterns, but the brothers didn't mind—far from it. Drawing attention to themselves was good publicity, and on any other night they would have encouraged the odd looks that their grade-B, horror movie costumes provoked, but tonight was different. Tonight was October 31st—Halloween—and in their business, the business of leading ghost-story walks through downtown Toronto, Halloween was the busiest night of the year. Their tour had been booked solid for weeks.

As the pair crossed the street, Dave commented, "That story Tim told us in the office this afternoon gave me the creeps."

"He's full of it," Andy, the older of the two, replied. "He was just trying to freak us out, to get us into character. What kind of idiots does he think we are? Yeah right—an angry vengeful spectre on the Halloween ghost tour? Sure, we're going to believe *that*, big guy."

"Don't you ever listen?" Dave asked accusingly as they crossed the street. "Tim didn't say it was Halloween that made the ghost appear. He said it was the full moon in October—the blood moon—that caused the haunting. It's only a coincidence that this year the full moon is on Halloween."

"Like I said, he's full of it. He's just being dramatic, is all. Hey, here's an idea—let's add his story about the demented ghost-guy to the script as we're walking people between sites."

Dave had time only to nod before they were standing at the foot of the museum's massive stone steps, surrounded by a crowd of people anxious to hear their scary stories. He usually loved everything about this moment, especially the feel of the crisp autumn air laced with the smell of fallen leaves. Tonight though, a sodden stillness hung about the group.

"Ladies and gentlemen, good Hallowed Eve to all of you, and welcome! My name is Dave and this is my brother Andy. We'll be leading you forth this evening as we brush the fragile veil that protects the world of the living from the world of the dead."

Andy took over their well-rehearsed script from there and proclaimed great admiration for anyone who joined a ghost walk on this particular evening—because although the tour would include a walk in the park, Queens Park that is, it would be filled with spine-chilling, one hundred percent true, carefully documented ghost stories. He gave a dramatic chuckle before adding, "There's even the possibility that the restless spirit of one long dead will join our tour. Yes, ladies and gentlemen, tonight you may see a ghost."

Giggles of anticipation ran through the crowd and Dave picked up the patter. "Gentle folk, pay heed to those words; if there's any one of you gathered here who would prefer to slip away alone into the cold and dark right now, *before* risking an encounter with the supernatural, then please, feel free to do so. We promise not to be offended. Not everyone can handle a glimpse through the curtain of time."

The brothers paused for a silent count of 10 while their audience shuffled from one foot to the other and looked around to see if anyone would walk away. Of course, no one ever did, and on the eleventh beat Andy asked, "Then we can assume that you're all anxious to risk a walk on the spirit side with us?"

When the customers called out "yes," as they always did in almost perfect unison, Dave lightened the tone by asking in mock horror, "Didn't your mothers ever tell you not to take walks with strangers? Folks, you should have listened to them because we might be the strangest strangers you'll ever meet! We're here to amaze, amuse and astonish you, and, while we're at it, we'll scare the jeepers out of at least a few of you. Your backbones could become icicles this evening!"

He gave a devilish laugh before flinging his cloak around his shoulders with a perfectly timed flourish that would have done Bela Lugosi proud. Then it was Andy's turn to speak—to tell everyone that it was time to start walking—but he didn't say a word. Dave prompted his brother with a nudge. As he did, a chilly draft blew between them, ruffling the folds of their cloaks.

"Huh? Oh yeah," Andy stumbled as though he'd been asleep. "Okay, it's time to walk to our first stop." But he didn't move. He stood utterly still and silent.

Annoyed, Dave improvised, announcing that even if the spirits didn't haunt them this evening, the ghost tour would visit places that were well and truly haunted. Then he leaned toward his brother and whispered, "What the heck is wrong with you? Get with it, would you?"

Andy didn't move. He stared straight ahead, frozen in place, fixated on a point just a little beyond the group.

"Loser, get with it," Dave said, and kicked at his brother's shoe.

"Dave, look!" Andy whispered. "That guy at the back… He's wearing an old-fashioned grey suit and a hat —a bowler hat. He's the one Tim told us about. See him? The bowler hat—he even has the cane with the gold handle like Tim said."

"You're crazy, man. It's Halloween. People dress up in costumes. Besides, I don't see any guy with a cane *or* a bowler hat. This is no time to be joking around. We're busy."

Andy blinked. The man's image had fragmented and then vanished completely. Nervously he shifted his lantern from one hand to the other and wrapped his cloak more tightly around his shoulders before picking up his part of the commentary. "Our first stop will be on the university campus. Let me assure you, this is a school with spirit, and that spirit's name is Ivan Reznikoff. His ghost has been haunting the campus since…"

Relieved that Andy's head was back in the game, Dave expelled a breath he hadn't known he'd been holding. This was a good-sized crowd, and handling the gig by himself would've been a pain because the two of them had perfected their routine over the previous weeks. When one was telling stories, the other would scan the crowd for potential trouble-makers. They didn't often get hecklers on the walk, but if there was one, it was always best to be aware in advance. Tonight everyone seemed intent on Andy's storytelling—a good sign. The additions to the introduction must have been effective.

"Reznikoff's ghost began appearing—" Andy suddenly stopped speaking as a single thick cloud scudded across the clear sky, blurring the full moon's silver-grey beams for just a moment.

Dave was startled too, but not by anything happening in the sky. He had felt a pocket of icy cold air right beside him. He swung around ready to shoo away a potential interloper, but there was no one there. It was odd because he could sense the person's presence. He looked again, but there was definitely no one there. *I guess it was just nerves from Tim's stupid story about there really being a ghost and Andy freezing there for a moment—plus a bit of closing night jitters. At least Andy is back on track.*

Resolving to do the best job possible, Dave waited for Andy to finish before relating another ghost story—a grisly tale of someone getting away with murder. Apparently two men who had been in business together had quarrelled viciously. When the disagreement became physical, the smaller of the two men had tried to flee but made it only as far as the emergency exit at the top of a steep exterior staircase. His opponent pushed him over the railing. The killer fled into the night, leaving his former partner to die on the gravel of the laneway below. The murdered man's soul was so tormented by this fatal injustice that it was unable to rest. A music producer was the last occupant of the building, and his story didn't end well either. He was forced out of business because no matter how he adjusted his expensive recording equipment, you could still hear ghostly cries for help in the background of every cut. "Now that the building is gone, I wonder where the ghost is," he concluded rhetorically.

A woman in the front row shivered in response, and Dave took advantage and played to her reaction by adding, "Why madam, you might just have felt that murdered man's spirit join us on this tour."

The words were barely out of his mouth when he noticed that the people at the back seemed unsettled, whispering among themselves and looking around. Dave stared in disbelief. A ghost had indeed joined them, but he knew it wasn't the soul of the murdered man. This was a much older spirit dressed in a grey wool suit and bowler hat, and there was no question that he wasn't human because Dave could see right through him. The transparent image wore an angry expression and shook a shiny black cane threateningly at the crowd. His eyes shone with hatred.

The brothers exchanged glances. They had both seen the apparition. The audience had clearly sensed that something was wrong, but they didn't seem to be able to see him.

Andy leaned closer to Dave. "Don't freak, man, it's only a reflection; that's why you can see through him. It's an image reflecting from the windows of the buildings. Ignore it. I'm just going to keep going."

People whispered uneasily to one another as Andy asked if there were any questions. There no doubt were questions—whoppers probably—but no one was willing to single themselves out from the safe anonymity of the crowd. The phantom, however, was getting more and more agitated. He waved his cane high in the air and seemed to be shouting—but mutely. Then the spectre fragmented, piece by piece, until it had dispersed entirely.

Thunder rumbled but the sky was clear. A cloud of warm, moist air rose from the grate on the sidewalk beside them. Dave looked down—it had only been a subway train leaving the station below them. The tour continued on, walking to the next stop.

Dave was relieved, but Andy wasn't because the apparition had reappeared and was staring directly at him. The image in the bowler hat wasn't just a reflection. It was a phantom, and an angry one too, judging by his expression. What classic irony: the Halloween tour was really haunted. Tim hadn't been slinging them a line after all. "I'm gonna get a normal job next year," he mumbled to himself as he stomped his feet to work off the anxiety that heaved in his gut.

Dave's neck muscles spasmed painfully. "It looks like no one else can see the ghost. Maybe it's because they don't know his story. Let's just get through this. We can cut it a bit short. It's not like anyone will know the difference."

"Yeah, I'm gonna tell the story about the ghost in the art gallery; then we'll cut it off." Andy cleared his throat before addressing the unsuspecting crowd. "So, ladies and gentlemen, this will be the last stop on our tour, but it's a good one. This grand old building you see before you was originally the home of a very wealthy Toronto family. As you can see, over the years there have been many dramatic changes made to the structure, but one aspect of it has remained consistent for at least 150 years and that is the ghost that haunts the place. No one knows who he is or why his spirit has never left, but people have seen his apparition clearly enough to describe him as a man dressed in a yellow waistcoat. Fortunately, there's no need to be afraid of this lost soul because he's certainly never hurt anyone—beyond scaring people half to death the first time they get a glimpse of his transparent image."

A few minutes later, the group was back at the museum's stone staircase where they had begun, and Andy was giving the closing patter.

"Are there any last minute questions?" the brothers asked in unison, hoping that their Halloween group was devoid of curiosity. No one had had a chance to speak before a gust of wind swirled grey ash throughout the crowd. A moment later, a hand-sized piece of gold-plated metal fell to the pavement at Dave and Andy's feet. It was the handle from an old-fashioned cane.

Roses Aren't Difficult Here

Even without her magnificent flower gardens Gloria would have been an institution in Smiths Falls. She was just a bride when she and her husband Russ had moved into that little cottage on the corner. By the mid-1950s, the clapboard bungalow was full to bursting with the couple's two happy, boisterous sons. Even at their rowdiest, though, the boys knew not to play on the west side of the front lawn. That area was reserved for their mother's rose garden, and it was a sight to behold every year. Neighbours waited for the blooms to appear and enjoyed the fragrance as it wafted gently through the air for those few weeks in summer. They all agreed: Gloria definitely had that special touch with roses.

Of course the kids eventually grew up and moved away, leaving Russ and Gloria alone in the cottage once again.

Suddenly finding herself with more time than ever to spend in her garden, Gloria let the roses take over more and more of the front lawn until the entire area in front of the bungalow was a riot of colour and fragrance. In summer even the tourists made a point to walk past Gloria's house. She liked to sit at the window, sipping her tea and watching their faces as they enjoyed the colourful array. It tickled her no end that her work seemed to bring delight to so many souls.

The only summer the blooms were ever neglected even a little was the year Russ died. People around town wondered if maybe she might sell the place and move into an apartment or a lodge, but Gloria knew where she belonged—at home, tending her garden.

Some neighbours thought that the roses gave the woman a reason to live while others thought it was simply the work of the gardening that kept her so strong and healthy. No one ever knew for certain, but for whatever reasons, Gloria lived a good long time. She was well into her nineties when she died peacefully.

Her sons, who had grown children of their own by then, quickly made their way back to Smiths Falls and the house where they were raised.

"According to Mom's instructions she wanted her body cremated," James, the older son, said as he and his brother stood in the kitchen they had loved as kids. "But she didn't say where she wanted her ashes spread."

Larry, the younger son, didn't respond to his brother's comments. He was rubbing his chin and looking out the window, at the west half of the front lawn and their mother's stupendous display of roses.

His silence annoyed James. "Earth to Larry. Are you there, Larry?"

"Yeah, I'm here. I'm just thinking. There's only one place that's reasonable to put Mom's ashes—in her garden. Remember how she always said that bone meal was the best fertilizer for roses?"

"That's not only disgusting but also illegal. I'm not having anything to do with your crazy idea," James declared.

"Fine. Then go back to the city and let me take care of things," Larry said as he escorted his brother to the side door. That night, after dark, he slipped outside, burial urn in hand, and scattered his mother's ashes over her beloved rose garden.

The next summer when Gloria's sons returned to Smiths Falls to sell their mother's little cottage, the rose blooms were even more spectacular than ever.

James laughed in spite of himself. "I've got to hand it to you. You did the right thing scattering Mom's ashes in the garden. Standing here I can just feel how happy her soul is. Sorry I hassled you about it."

"You were partly right, though," Larry replied. "What I did was illegal. We'd better keep this our secret."

When they called the local real estate office to list their mother's house for sale, the agent said he had good news. He had just been talking to a family wanting to move to town. They were specifically looking for a corner lot that size and were willing to pay full value. The agent paused before adding, "Of course, your mother's house is old by now. These people, they'll want to tear it down and build their own."

Larry and James were taken aback at first, but the more they thought about it, the more reasonable the agent's news sounded. It was James who spoke first. "Before we go ahead, can you have the buyers come around and speak to us?"

"That won't be a problem. They'll want to see the lot anyway, I'm sure."

A few hours later, a car pulled up in front of the house. The couple was delighted with the property and wanted to buy it immediately.

Larry looked at James, then at the couple. "We do have one special request. We'd like you to keep the rose garden exactly as it is."

The woman smiled and nodded. "Of course we'll keep those roses. They're glorious!"

"Yes," James agreed. "They are. They are Gloria's."

A Certain Look

"Are you gentlemen ready to order?" the waiter asked with obvious disinterest.

Terry turned to the young man on his left. "Decided on anything, son?"

"Not yet," Carl said and looked across the table at his brother, who seemed to be staring off into space far beyond the Napanee restaurant where they were sitting. "Eddie, you order first."

There was no reply.

"Ed, I said you go first. You gonna have the special?"

Terry glanced from one of his sons to the other. Carl looked mildly annoyed, which wasn't unusual when he was with his younger brother, but Eddie looked terrible. Beads of sweat dotted his forehead, he was pale and his eyes were glassy. Was he getting a migraine? It had been years since the kid had endured one of those, but in his teens he had been tormented by headaches. He always got that certain look about him just before the pain hit. How long since he'd had one? Five years maybe? Everyone figured he'd outgrown them.

"Eddie!" the older man's concern about his younger son put such an edge in his voice that Carl was taken aback. Their father usually didn't sound stern like that; he was a pretty easy-going guy.

"Huh?" Eddie looked at his father and brother. "I can't even think about food. Look over there at that guy, the one at the corner table with the red sweatshirt on. He's freaky, man. Worse than freaky."

Carl followed his younger brother's stare to a darkened table in the corner of the restaurant, where a heavy-set man wearing an oversized red sweatshirt sat by himself. The guy certainly wasn't eye-candy, but calling him "freaky" was a bit much. Carl glanced at his father; the older man's eyebrows were raised. No one spoke.

"I'll give you a couple more minutes, then," the waiter said and shuffled away.

"Dad, do something!" Eddie urged in a stage whisper.

"What? Do something about what?" Terry asked, sounding confused.

"About that guy being in here! It's disgraceful. A dead guy should *not* be in a restaurant." Eddie's voice was shrill, verging on panic.

"A dead guy?" Terry asked.

Carl impatiently shoved his cutlery to the side. "Knock it off, stupid, and just order your food. I'm hungry."

"But how can you be hungry when you can see that… that…*thing*?"

Terry sighed. That afternoon he'd been berating himself for not taking his sons out for dinner more often, but this wasn't working out well at all. "Ed, are you all right? If you're not, please say so, but if you're okay then either tell us what we're supposed to be seeing or drop the nonsense."

Eddie put the palms of his hands on the table and spoke slowly. "The guy in the corner over there can't be alive. They must have him propped up somehow. Look at him. His face is covered in blood, and half his skull is smashed in. And his shirt is all ripped and filthy. How did they let anyone bring him in here? I'm calling the police."

Terry looked toward the corner table and then back at his son. He put his hand on Eddie's shoulder. "It's just the dim lighting over there in the corner—too many shadows. It's too dark in the whole place if you ask me, but who cares? The guy's getting up to leave anyway."

Carl nodded. "Yeah, the dude's going, Eddie, so snap out of it. Come on, let's just order our dinner, okay? I'm hungry and I want to be home in time to watch the game. It's Argos at Ti' Cats. Should be a good one."

Eddie took a deep breath and muttered, "Yeah, I guess whatever the waiter said was the special of the day sounded all right. Order for me, okay? I'm going to the men's room to throw some cold water on my face."

After the young man walked away, Terry held up his hand to signal the waiter. Just then a tremendous thump reverberated through the restaurant. Diners, including Terry and Carl, jumped up from their tables and ran to the window.

The guy who had been sitting at the corner table had stepped off the curb in front of a truck. His red-sweatshirted, heavy-set body had flown like a rag-doll until the side of his head slammed against a concrete pole and he died.

Terry turned to his son. "Carl, get Eddie. Take him out the back door. I'll bring the car around."

The Same Silly Spooky Story

Rebecca knew she should have headed out earlier than she had, but it had been so long since she had seen her sister and brother-in-law, and they had all been having so much fun visiting, that it was impossible to have any regrets. Besides, she was on her way home to Brockville now and it was a perfect night for a drive.

The first few kilometres would be a bit slow—unpaved country roads and all—but she could just enjoy the gorgeous harvest moon hanging like an orange-coloured disc in the cloudless sky. Once she turned onto the highway she would be home in no time.

It was cold but there hadn't been any snow yet, which meant that there wasn't even as much as a flicker of reflected light. Rebecca had forgotten just how dark it was at night in the countryside. Those bare fields swallowed every sliver of light the moonbeams offered.

Too bad the car radio wasn't working. Hearing a human voice would have eased Rebecca's sense of isolation. Well, any human voice except her wacky brother-in-law Ben's voice. He was such a character. He just never changed, that one. He had been telling her the same spooky story for 10 years. Would he ever catch on that she wasn't a little kid anymore like she was when he started dating Miranda?

At least this time he tried to put some variety into his tired old campfire story by changing the details from "a mad man named Walter roaming the area" to "the ghost of a mad man named Walter roaming the area." And of course he always ended with his most sincere tone of voice saying, "I'm not kidding, you know, Rebecca. Honestly I'm not."

Ha ha, very inventive, Ben. Not.

Her brother-in-law had also told Rebecca that she should trade in this old wreck of a car she had been driving since she was 16 and get herself a newer one. He was probably right about that. The old heap just wasn't holding up anymore. Mechanically it still hadn't given her any trouble, but she had actually felt embarrassed when Miranda and

Ben had seen the car. She had tried to make a joke of it, but it was pretty obvious they were both concerned when they saw her using the passenger's door to get into the car because the driver's door was jammed. And the fenders— they were almost rusted away. *Oh well*, she thought. *Nothing I can do about that right now.*

Rebecca shifted a bit in her seat. She realized she'd been clenching her teeth. This total darkness was definitely a strain. She was relieved to see that the highway was just around the next curve. The steady flow of traffic looked comforting after feeling so alone on the dark country road. No more than a minute or two away now there would be people and cars around her, and the other cars' headlights would help penetrate the darkness.

It was a good thing, too. The knots in her neck muscles were screaming for relief. She wiggled her shoulders to shake off the tension, but the movement must have changed the angle of her right leg because the car slowed as though she had eased off the gas. She flexed her foot more firmly on the pedal. The car shuddered and backfired before jerking to a stop in a dead stall.

Rebecca cursed. *Stupid old wreck of a car didn't even make it to the highway. Okay, okay, take a breath, keep calm. There's no danger, no cars coming. You can get the car started again. This is just a fluke; it's never happened before.*

Rebecca twisted the key in the ignition until it cut into her finger. The engine was dead. *It's still okay—phone Miranda and Ben. They'll come get me.*

Rebecca fumbled for her phone and cursed again. Her phone was dead. She wasn't Catholic, but she crossed herself anyway. The gesture wasn't nearly enough though to ward off her tears of fear and frustration at the sinking realization that she was stranded at night on a country road near a busy highway. Sobs wracked her body so violently that the car wobbled.

Calm down, she told herself. *You're so panicked you're shaking the car! Be still, be still and breathe.* Finally the young woman's instructions to herself began to take effect. *Thanks be for those yoga classes,* she thought an instant before looking up at the dual headlights of a transport truck bearing down on her, its cab and trailer jackknifing in a deadly, oversized game of crack-the-whip. Paralyzed by fear, Rebecca watched in helpless horror until an odd calmness descended over her. It was as though she had no fear left in her. There was nothing more she could do anyway. She rested her head on the back of the seat and waited for the impact.

But there wasn't a crash. There wasn't any noise at all. The car simply lurched to the right. *Odd.* That was Rebecca's final thought before slumping in a dead faint.

Slowly consciousness percolated through her brain. She opened her eyes and looked around. Blackness enveloped her. Was she dead? She didn't feel dead, but maybe she was.

"Hang tough, missy," a man's voice penetrated the blackness. The Grim Reaper? "We'll have you out of there in no time. That was some pretty fancy driving you did to get out of the transport's way in time. Poor guy had a heart attack. He's a goner—not even a pulse left."

Rebecca nodded. What had just happened? She could barely remember. She was pretty sure she wasn't dead. She'd need a new car for certain now, but at least she wasn't dead. Some truck driver was, though, poor soul. People came running toward her. From where?

"We've gotta pry your driver's side door off, ma'am. The way you landed here in the culvert, there's just no other way," someone said.

Rebecca turned her head toward the voice. Her mind was beginning to function a bit better. One of these people must have called for help. She had to call Miranda and Ben. The ringing phone would scare them silly, but she needed them to get her away from all the noise around her, all the breaking, ripping, tearing and crunching metal that was assaulting her ears.

Then, slowly, she felt herself being pulled free of the car. Someone wrapped her in a blanket and carried her to the seat of a pick-up truck. Rebecca took a deep breath and sat up. She was okay—not even bruised.

Sirens screamed in the distance. More and more people milled around, asking if she was all right. "Does anyone have a phone?" she asked, and half a dozen hands holding phones were thrust toward her. She took the nearest one, but her hands were shaking too badly to hit the tiny buttons accurately.

"Let me help you, dear," a woman's voice offered. "You have no idea how lucky you were tonight. Did you even realize that today is the anniversary of Walter's death?"

Walter? Walter? Who's Walter? The name is familiar. Oh right, now she remembered. Rebecca sighed at the silliness of it all, especially considering the situation. Walter is the name of the silly spooky guy Ben always talked about.

Unbelievably, the woman kept on about the dumb urban legend. "He escaped from the institution years ago, you know, and from then on lived as a hermit, hiding away in the forest. Of course folks always knew when he was around. Some even caught glimpses of him and there'd be vegetables missing from their gardens and the like. A few neighbours took to leaving food and blankets out for him. Then last year he just wandered out onto the highway. He was hit by a semi—full on. To this day no one knows if he was just confused or actually trying to kill himself. It was so sad; the first actual look any of us had of him was when he was lying dead right by this exact intersection. I don't mind telling you, I was one of those who came out and had a look at him. Shocked, that's what I was. Shocked by the size of him. The man was enormous; he had huge hands."

Rebecca sat motionless on the seat of the truck, dumbfounded by what she been told. The world around her slipped into the distance.

From somewhere far away, the man who'd pulled her out of the car spoke. "I've gotta tell you missy, your car is totalled. The right rear fender has been torn clear off. I brought the piece up from the gully, though I don't rightly know why I did. It's sure not worth anything. But it looks for all the world like some big old pair of hands just grabbed that thing and pulled at it, like he wanted to toss the whole car off the road. We might never know exactly what happened here tonight, but whatever it was, it happened just in the nick of time. You would have been killed for sure."

Saving Grace

Ten-year-old Grace looked around the tiny room. She'd never been in a teacher's washroom before, and now that she was, she was seriously disappointed. A toilet, a sink and a window covered with wire mesh. She'd gone to a lot of trouble to get in here, and it had *so* not been worth it.

If the questions in the math workbook hadn't been as boring as they were then maybe Grace wouldn't have been so restless. The teacher had been busy at the back of the classroom and her classmates all had their heads down, working on math problems. A big, shiny set of keys hung on a hook just inside the classroom door. Quietly, Grace got up from her desk.

Seconds later she was at the door of the teachers' washroom across the hall. Kids were never allowed in there—well, except that spoiled brat Mary Beth, who'd supposedly sprained her ankle last winter and couldn't manage her crutches well enough to get from the top floor to the girls' washroom in the basement. Grace had wanted to see the forbidden place ever since.

Each key on the teacher's key ring had a tag on it to tell which door it opened, so Grace had no trouble getting into the room, but she'd barely had time to look around before a bell rang. It couldn't be recess time already, could it? No, the recess bell only rang for a few seconds. This horrible noise kept on and on. The little girl's heart sank. This was the signal for a fire drill.

Students and teachers poured out of classrooms silently and in straight rows. Grace was trapped. Someone was sure to notice her if she came out of the teacher's bathroom now, and that would mean at least a week of detentions. Her only chance to avoid getting caught was to stay exactly where she was until the three "all clear" bells sounded. She'd been through enough school fire drills to know that coming back into the building was a lot more chaotic than going out. She could just slip into the middle of a group heading back into the classroom. No one would ever have to know where she'd been. Yeah, that's what she'd do.

The "all clear" signal couldn't happen fast enough for Grace. It seemed like she'd been hidden away by herself forever. Her head ached and she was dizzy. She felt like she did last June at field day after she'd been standing out in the sun all afternoon. Was she going to throw up? She couldn't—not in a *teachers'* toilet.

Why didn't the fire bell stop? The noise was horrible. It made her head hurt even more. Wait—she knew why the alarm didn't stop. This wasn't a fire drill. This was a fire. Grace reached for the doorknob. Where was it? Why couldn't she find it? Thick smoke filled the room. She tried to scream. It hurt to breathe. She gagged back a cough just before crumbling to the floor.

"You've given yourself quite a bump on the head, young lady. We'll have to get that fixed up, but first we need to get you outside with the others, don't we?"

A man's voice spoke to her from somewhere off in the distance. She felt herself being lifted from the cold tile floor and carried down the stairs and out to the schoolyard. She didn't recognize the man, but he must have known who she was because he set her down in the midst of all the others from her class. She looked up to say thank you, but she couldn't see him. No wonder—there were firemen everywhere. *This* was way more interesting than math *or* the teachers' washroom! Grace had been right; this was no fire drill. This was the real thing.

"Gracie, what happened? Sit down, you've really cut yourself. Your head's bleeding." Her teacher's voice sounded scared. "Here, take my jacket and press it to your forehead. I'll get the nurse."

Over the next few days, news of the emergency was all over the Kitchener newspaper and television stations. They said that the fire itself hadn't done much damage, but that the smoke had been dangerous. Had anyone stayed in the building, especially on the top floor, they would have suffocated. But all that mattered to Grace was that no one ever found out she'd been in the teacher's bathroom.

The next week when school started again, the principal called an assembly. He went on and on about how proud he was of the way everyone had acted during the emergency. While he talked, Grace stared at the pictures on the wall behind him. She had never looked very closely at them before, but something about one of them had caught her eye. One of the photos was of the man who had carried her downstairs the day of the fire!

Grace tugged at her teacher's sleeve and whispered, "Who's that man in the picture right behind where the principal is standing?"

"Shhhh," her teacher warned her, but then added, "That's Mr. Jacobsen. You won't know him. He was the principal here in the 1950s."

I Can Take You...

"If we could have your attention, please, for the safety announcement…"

No you can't, Jill thought, fixing her earplugs in place. *I need to sleep way more than I need to listen to your safety announcement. I'll nap for an hour and you'll fly me safely to Sudbury; how's that for a deal?*

Minutes later the world of business meetings, profit margins and downsizing had lost its intensity as Jill began to drift away into the sanctuary of sleep. She knew the world of the corporate ladder; she'd climbed it two rungs at a time. This afternoon's schedule would require her full-on corporate self, and after this week's stressful schedule, she needed a power nap to get back in the game.

The drone of the plane's engines soothed Jill into unconsciousness. She began dreaming of a ladder—not the corporate ladder, though. Her dream ladder was the kind of ladder you find in a playground, on a little kids' slide…

What fun! It had been years since Jill had been in a playground. She climbed the metal steps to the top of the slide and looked down. It was a long way down—a really long way. This slide was awfully high for a piece of kids' playground equipment. Weird. It was way higher than it should have been for the height of the ladder. How could that be? How could something be farther down than it was up? It didn't make any sense.

Now there was someone at the bottom of the slide. Where did he come from? Who was he? He was kinda cute—well, in a boyish kind of way. Wait, that's Jake Gyllenhaal, the actor! But that's ridiculous. It couldn't be him. For one thing he's older than that now. That's about how old he looked in Brokeback Mountain. *Those sure weren't his* Brokeback Mountain *clothes, though. Why would he be dressed like that, like he was a doorman at a hotel, for goodness sake. Maybe he was in costume. No, it just couldn't be him. Darn, though, that really did look like him at the bottom of the slide.*

He caught Jill's eye and smiled at her. Awful. That couldn't be Jake; that was a ghastly smile and Jake had a great smile. This guy's smile was dripping nasty.

"Come on," the Jake Gyllenhaal look-alike said. It wasn't an invitation. It was a command.

Jill turned to flee but caught her heel on a metal rung near the top of the ladder and fell headlong to the hard, packed earth below. Pain shot through the left side of her crumpled body. She whimpered and looked around. The young Jake Gyllenhaal's leering image was right there, smiling menacingly at her. She tried to scramble away but something held her in place.

"I'm hurt," Jill pleaded. "I need to get to a hospital."

"*Come on. I can take you,*" he said. *There was no reassurance in his voice at all. His statement was a threat.*

Jill woke with a start. She looked around. She wasn't in a playground at all. She was on a plane, of course, a plane that had just landed in Sudbury. That was what had wakened her, the touch down. Everything was all right. She was where she was supposed to be. *How embarrassing, having a nightmare on a plane. I sure am glad I didn't have a seatmate. I hope I didn't talk in my sleep.*

Jill's fellow passengers seemed blissfully unaware of the unconscious trauma she had just been through. She smiled to herself, realizing why she had dreamt that something held her in place. It was the seat belt. Her left side ached. She had wedged herself against the plane's window as far as her fastened seat belt would allow.

I need to get off this plane, she thought as the aircraft slowed to a stop. She wished she had time to walk off the effects of her dream, but there was barely enough time to drop her suitcase at the hotel before she had to be at the office.

When the fasten seat belt light went off, Jill stood up immediately so she could at least stretch her legs while she waited for the plane's doors to open. Ten minutes later she stood in the sunshine on the sidewalk in front of the airport, checking the line-up of hotel shuttle buses.

There it is, the blue one. That's the one for my hotel. She caught the driver's eye, nodded to him and, pulling her suitcase, walked toward the blue bus. *I had better ask the guy first, though, just to make sure.*

"Come on. I can take you," he told her in response to her question.

His voice, even his words, were familiar—familiar and foreboding. Jill looked into the darkened bus. A young Jake Gyllenhaal look-alike sat in the driver's seat, sneering back at her. She turned to flee but her suitcase was at her feet. She tripped and fell headlong onto the cement. Pain shot down the left side of her crumpled body. She'd broken her arm. That much she knew for certain.

The First Cottage

Hank slid off the stool behind the counter, pulled the window curtain aside and peered out into the inky blackness. The colours of the neon sign at the end of his driveway blinked as the sheets of rain washed over it and the rest of the landscape for kilometres around. There hadn't been many cars on that road all day, and those who had passed certainly hadn't stopped in to take a room. He'd give it another half-hour before turning off the "Vacancy" sign and settling in for the evening to listen to the radio and smoke his pipe.

Lots of people thought that once the war was over Hank would get on with his life, but he'd been a civilian again for nearly five years now, and it was clear that the war had shelled any ambition he might ever have had straight out of him. Not one of the veterans' grants he could have taken advantage of would have deterred Hank from his quiet existence tending the small motor court just outside Gravenhurst. "God's country," he always called it. The area's beauty and isolation would always be more than enough for him.

The rain beat a soothing rhythm against the window-panes, and Hank relaxed into his chair and let his mind wander back to the sunny, summer days of his youth, swimming in the crystal clear lakes and rivers, hiking through the untouched woodlands…

A sharp sound jolted him awake. He jumped to his feet, adrenaline racing through his body. Gunfire! What direction? No, no, it's okay. Everything is all right—it wasn't gunfire at all, only a customer who had come into the motel office and wrapped his knuckles on the counter to get Hank's attention. Even so, it took Hank a few seconds to realize not only that the man meant no harm but also that he was drenched to the bone from head to toe and needed help.

"Sorry to startle you," he told Hank. "It seems that I've done something stupid. Can you let me have a room for the night? I was trying to make it home, and I guess I was driving too fast for the wet roads because I didn't quite make it around that last turn in the road. I just slid off into the culvert."

"You all right?" Hank asked, examining the drenched man's dejected appearance.

"I'm fine, just mad at myself. The car is a goner. Darned shame. It was brand new and an absolute beauty: a dark blue, four-door Mercury. Barely had a hundred kilometres on 'er."

Hank winced with compassion at the man's situation. That *would* be humiliating, to drive your new car off the road and end up at some stranger's door all wet and cold, covered in mud. No wonder he looked so ashamed—like the life had been sucked right out of him.

Hank tried to reassure the man. "Well, there's no hope of getting that car winched out of there till morning, but at least your timing was good. I was about to close up here. You never would've found me without that sign of mine being on. Make yourself at home in the first cottage. It's not locked. There should be plenty of hot water for a shower, and a stock of clean towels and blankets. In the morning when the rain's stopped we'll get a tow truck out here."

The next morning, Hank was still fast asleep on his cot in the back room when he heard someone calling. Then he remembered the traveller from the night before, the one who booked in because he had driven his car off the road. He pulled his suspenders up over his shoulders and hurried to the counter.

A young police officer from town stood with his arm outstretched to greet the innkeeper. "Sorry to bother you, Hank, but I need to use your phone. There's been an accident at that last turn in the road. I need to get a tow truck and the boys from the morgue out here."

Hank indicated the phone perched at the end of the counter. "Help yourself. I know about the wreck, but you don't need anybody from the morgue. The guy who was driving that car checked in here last night."

"Driving the new four-door Mercury?"

"Yeah, that's what he said. He was sure mad at himself, too. He told me the car was pretty much brand new."

"I've got bad news for you, Hank. The guy who drove off the road last night is still behind the wheel, and he's colder than last week's pickerel."

"No, he's not," Hank argued. "I talked to him. He stayed the night in the first cottage over there. He's still there, for that matter. I'm sure he'll be along here anytime now. He was pretty concerned about that new car of his."

The officer shot Hank an odd look before calling the telephone operator in Gravenhurst to get her to round up the people he would need to get the accident cleaned up.

Hank wandered outside. The rain had stopped. It was still cool, but the sun was shining and the birds were chirping. He breathed deeply as he knocked on the door of the first cottage. The guy must have been so dog tired from the accident last night that he didn't hear Hank knocking.

I'd better get him up if they're going to pull his car out, Hank thought, and turned the doorknob.

A path of muddy shoe prints trailed across the floor from the door to the bed—and then stopped. There was no one on the bed. There was no one in the room. It was as neat and tidy as it had been when Hank himself had cleaned it the week before.

Not a living soul had come into the first cottage since then.

The Figurines

Keith was confused—confused and annoyed and discouraged. Sandra, the easy-going, bright, bubbly woman he'd loved madly during the two years they'd dated seemed to have vaporized, only to reappear as a prissy pain-in-the-butt. And all of this change had happened since their wedding last June. Worse, the transformation had changed her from the most appealing woman he'd ever met to being a solid contender for someone he wouldn't even have been interested in taking to lunch, let alone marrying. The thought that he'd never feel the tightness of her arms around his waist as he gunned the Kawasaki through northern Ontario's backroads made him sad beyond measure, but more and more, that was exactly the way things were looking.

What had happened? Where was the woman whose favourite outfit used to be hiking boots and climbing shorts? That's the Sandra he'd married, and for the life of him, Keith couldn't figure out what had happened to her. Where had she gone?

That question was valid on another level; she was hardly ever home these days. Last year at this time Keith could have guaranteed that if they weren't at work, they would absolutely have been together. Now he rarely saw her. She always had places to go, and they were never places for the two of them. On Saturdays she took interior decorating seminars, and two evenings a week she had party planning classes. Then, just when Keith had thought there'd be a blank spot in her schedule, she'd signed up for a gourmet cooking workshop. It was like she was determined to transform herself into some weird image of what she thought a wife should be. It was all very 1950s.

Keith rubbed his eyes in an attempt to staunch the wicked headache building at his temples. It wasn't just Sandra who was changing; the house was looking different too. Up until a few months ago, their place had been decorated (if you could even call it "decorated") in a minimalist style. Now each day it was getting more and more cluttered. Those stupid silk plants she'd insisted on buying—they were all over the house. What the heck was with those? They were pricey too. Who would have guessed?

The worst for expensive, though, were those ghastly china figurines. Those things were just a stupid price; plus, it seemed Sandra could never have enough of the darned things. They already covered the entire table in the corner of the living room. She must have a thousand dollars invested in them already—if not more. What a waste of money that could have been spent on fun, like a scuba diving trip for the two of them.

But there was no end to this nonsense in sight because now she was jonesing after even more figurines—although maybe that was a good idea, especially if one of them was big enough to hide that ugly umbrella-lady ornament. That one seriously creeped Keith out. There was something about the set of her mouth—it was like she was smirking. And those cold, hard china eyes—they seemed to be staring right at him no matter where he was in the room.

Just thinking about the stupid ornaments had given him a headache so bad he was actually starting to feel queasy. He lowered himself heavily into the easy chair behind him, thinking that Sandra had better not try to move his chair out of the living room, even if it didn't fit her new image of how the house should look. Maybe the place hadn't looked perfect, but then neither were they, and that was the way he wanted things.

Not like those figurines with their tiny, shiny perfection. Take that ugly umbrella lady as an example. Her umbrella wasn't open and above her head because that would have implied less than perfect weather. No, she was holding the thing closed with the tip resting just beside her absolutely flawless miniature right shoe.

Keith leaned his head back and closed his eyes. At least that way he couldn't see the dumb figurine—even if it could still see him. The utter irrationality of that thought jolted him upright, his eyes wide open. He stared at the ornament. He'd never noticed before, but she wasn't just holding her umbrella, she was leaning on it like a cane. *Hah—maybe you're not so perfect after all, little knick-knack —not if you're grimacing and using your accessory as a prop. Look around you at your fellow figurines. They're perfect and you're not! Hah.*

He squinted to look more closely at the umbrella lady. Now he saw it. He'd been wrong. She wasn't grimacing at all. That wasn't pain in her expression. It was anger in her horrid, glistening, tiny, painted-on eyes. The air in the room turned frigid. Keith shuddered.

Why was the thing so near the edge of the table? He hadn't remembered her being that close to him, but now that she *was* closer, he realized she wasn't leaning on the umbrella at all—as a matter of fact, the pointy end was actually raised up from her smooth porcelain base. The umbrella was pointing at him, menacing him.

Bile oozed from Keith's stomach to his throat. He pushed himself farther back in the chair. This was no ordinary china ornament—ordinary china ornaments don't threaten people. *Oh god Sandra, get home and call this thing off!*

Umbrella lady knew. She knew that he'd caught on, that she was coming for him. Lowering the tip of the umbrella back down to her china base, the ornament pivoted and moved itself even closer to him. Keith could smell her sour, hate-filled breath. A spasm of fear jolted through his body. He slumped forward in a faint.

And that's where Sandra found him when she came home a few minutes later. He was cold and clammy and muttering incoherently about the figurines.

"You must have fallen asleep and had a bad dream," she told him as his eyelids fluttered open. "There's nothing wrong with my figurines."

Keith looked over at the ornaments. She was right, of course. There was nothing wrong with them. A shiver ran through him.

Sandra glanced at him and suggested that it looked like he might be getting the flu or something, so maybe they should just rent a movie and stay home this evening.

Keith nodded gratefully and then added, "We could order take-out and watch the movie while we're eating."

"Eat dinner here in the living room? Are you completely crazy?" The shrill edge to her voice made Keith wince. "What if we get crumbs on the new couch?"

Keith sighed. Just before closing his eyes he looked over at the table full of ornaments. The umbrella lady had that smirk on her face again.

What a Celebration

"What a celebration that was yesterday," Wilf said to his wife as she poured their morning tea.

Anne nodded. "Wasn't that something? I can't believe all those folks came to see us on our wedding anniversary. Almost the whole town of Belleville showed up."

"People kept saying it was such a great accomplishment, staying married for 65 years, but you know, it honestly doesn't seem that way to me. I can't imagine my life any other way than with you," Wilf declared, looking over at his wife. She was looking tired, but that was really no wonder. It had been a long time since they had had so much excitement in one day, but the party had been *so* much fun—definitely a moment to remember for the rest of their lives. He was feeling a bit worn out himself.

"It was too bad that Agnes and Stan Bentley weren't there," Anne said, stirring sugar into her tea.

Wilf looked up in surprise. "But Anne, you know they've been dead for years."

For a moment, silence hung in the air between the two. Then Anne stood up, turned her back to her husband and walked to the kitchen sink. "I know that!" she snapped. Her voice could still get as feisty as it had when she was a girl. "Still, what I said is true. It's too bad the Bentleys weren't at the party. They would have enjoyed it. That's all I meant."

Wilf watched his wife as she stood staring out the kitchen window. He had noticed that her mind wasn't as sharp as it had once been. Sometimes he wondered if he was slipping too. Probably so. One thing was certain, though: the party had been wonderful, but they were both exhausted. They needed to rest.

Wilf knew from experience that he would have to word his suggestion of a nap very carefully. Anne was still a bit prickly from his having pointed out her error about the Bentleys. "I have to tell you, I could do with a bit of a nap," he said quietly. "Would you come and lie down with me?"

Anne turned to look at her husband. There had been no need to snap at him. It wasn't really him she was annoyed with. It was herself. What had made her say such a stupid thing about the Bentleys? They had been to both Stan's and Agnes's funerals, for goodness sake. She looked more carefully at her husband. He did look tired. She nodded. "Even if we don't fall asleep, we could just lie quietly for a while. That would be restful. Maybe afterward we could go for a walk around the block. It's a beautiful spring day. The kind we always enjoy."

Hand in hand, the elderly couple walked slowly to their bedroom and, without even turning down the faded blue chenille bedspread, lay down.

Wilf was the first to wake. He looked over at the woman he had married when he'd been a young man of 22 and she just a few months younger. She looked like an angel lying there, sleeping so peacefully. Taking that nap had been a wise thing to do. He felt so much better now, and he knew Anne would too. He rolled over to stare out the window at the perfectly blue, cloudless sky. The small movement woke Anne.

"Sorry," he said. "I didn't mean to wake you."

Anne smiled. "I was waking up anyway. I feel so much better than I did when we lay down. Let's go for that walk."

The two made their way outside to the sidewalk. "It's like a summer's day," Anne said.

Wilf smiled. His wife was right, but mostly he was happy to hear so much energy back in her voice.

A small boy rode past on a bicycle, waved at them and called, "Hello to you both!"

"Do we have new neighbours?" Wilf asked. "I don't recognize that lad."

"He looked so much like little Jimmy, the Randalls' boy, but of course it can't be. He died years ago in that awful car accident," Anne said, taking a deep breath.

Wilf reached down and clasped Anne's hand in his. They had always liked holding hands. As they rounded the corner at the end of the block, they saw a woman hanging clothes out to dry on a backyard clothesline.

Wilf gasped. "That's Agnes!" he exclaimed.

"You old fool," Anne teased. "We've already talked about Stan and Agnes today."

"Let's turn around. Let's go back home. Quickly. Please. I don't want her to see us. I'm sure that's Agnes Bentley. There's something wrong here, very wrong. We need to go back home, right now."

Anne nodded, but she had to admit she was a little disappointed. She would have loved a visit with Agnes, dead or not—the two women had always had the most interesting conversations—but it was clear that Wilf was upset. It would be all right though; as soon as they got home he would settle down in his favourite chair to read the newspaper, and then she could slip away by herself for a chat with Agnes. That would be more satisfying anyway. She could wrap up some of the leftovers from the party last night and take them to her friend. It was strange that neither she nor Stan was there for the celebration.

Wilf was scared. His body felt a bit odd, lighter somehow. All he wanted was to get to the comfort of his own home. As he and Anne came to their front yard, the lilac bush shook and Goldie, the wonderful cocker spaniel they had had while the kids had been growing up, ran up to greet them. How they had all loved that dog. They had all been so sad when she died. Goldie had been an important member of the family.

Wilf sighed. He felt good now—never felt better, actually. He looked over at Anne. She was as beautiful as always, a shimmering image of light. He smiled as he felt his body break apart, splinter into tiny, shining particles. He reached for Anne's hand.

The Last Vampire

Warren stood quietly watching his daughter as she sat at the kitchen table reading. So much had changed over the years—Norah was a young woman now—but much had also remained the same because she'd always loved to read scary books, and the kitchen was still her favourite room. Smiling, the man set a pot of water to boil on the stove.

Norah looked up from her book and out into the darkened yard beyond the window. Had something moved outside? Was something in the yard? A person? Could be, the height was about right, but a person couldn't possibly stand like that—not so still and upright.

The young woman rubbed her eyes and looked again, with relief this time. The breeze from Lake Simcoe must have blown a piece of black cloth against the fence. That's all it was. She should stop reading so many horror stories. Her imagination was obviously way too active because she could have sworn that the first time she looked out she'd seen a tall, thin man wrapped in a black cloak standing very, very still just outside the window.

"Making tea?" she asked her father, more from the desire for some familiar and comforting human contact than from any need for information.

He turned away from the stove and nodded. "I need to run upstairs for a second. Could you please pour the water into the pot when you hear the kettle whistle?"

Norah nodded absently until a noise at the back door startled her. She looked up. That hadn't been any sort of material blown by the breezes from the lake. She was face to face with a tall, thin, black-cloaked figure. It stared at her with yellow eyes. And then it pounced.

Warren heard his daughter cry out. He took the stairs three at a time, but he was too late. Norah lay unconscious, a black-cloaked figure kneeling over her. A putrid stench filled the air. The thing ran from the house, but not before looking at Warren for just a second—just long enough for him to see its yellow eyes.

Norah's face and throat were slashed. She was bleeding profusely. At the hospital the doctor worked feverishly on the young woman's wounds, stitching them as best he could, all the while silently speculating on what sort of an animal could have wrought such damage. He would certainly have to report this attack to the authorities, but what to say? Who or what had been her assailant? Was there a rabid dog loose somewhere? But he knew no cur was responsible for this assault. He'd seen hundreds of dog bites in his time, and these were far worse.

The injured girl was still heavily sedated when her father brought her home from the hospital later that night. Over the next few days, word of the terrifying incident

spread throughout the community. People worried—
would Norah ever be the same? What could have muti-
lated her so viciously and left her so terrified?

The wounds on Norah's body healed, but even weeks
later the mental and emotional scars from the attack
remained raw. She refused to be anywhere alone. Warren
did what he could for his daughter, but still she suffered
terribly. It was becoming obvious that the young woman
would never be the same.

As days became weeks and weeks turned into months,
people's attention wandered. Occasionally a neighbour
would drop by to see how the two of them were doing, but
that was about all. One day, a man Warren barely knew
paid a call.

"I'm sorry about what happened to your daughter," the
man said.

Norah's father nodded and thanked the man for his
concern but added, "It's past us now. Dwelling on it does
no good."

"If I may speak freely, I have something to say that you
should interest you."

Warren shrugged his shoulders impatiently but stayed
where he was in the doorway to listen to what the man
had to say.

"You should know that your daughter's was not the
first assault of this kind. It was many years ago, but a few
around here still remember. The girl who was attacked
said that the beast was hideous beyond belief. When it
came after her a second time there were people nearby

who gave chase to the beast. They followed it to near the old burial grounds before they lost sight of it."

"I thank you for your trouble in coming here this evening, but really, with all due respect sir, this is 1970. No one believes that sort of nonsense anymore," Norah's father declared.

The men stared awkwardly at one another before the neighbour turned to walk away.

Warren called out after him, "What about the girl? Did she ever recover?"

"No one knows. The family moved away. They feared that once the beast had a taste of the girl's blood, she wouldn't be safe in the area," he replied. And then he left.

Norah's father leaned against the wall for support. Just the other evening he'd seen something out in the yard, something he'd hoped was a pair of fireflies—yellow fireflies with veins of red running through their bodies. Now he knew he'd only been fooling himself. The beast was back, stalking, planning for his next feed.

Warren armed himself with his hunting rifle and stood in the room where Norah had been attacked. Hours later his patience was rewarded. Just outside the window, a black-cloaked shadow darkened the evening landscape. Warren fired a shot and the thing fell—but only for an instant. Then it was up and running away at full speed. The man followed, screaming curses and threats. Neighbours heard the racket and came running.

The mob followed the monster through the moonlit night to a crumbling vault in the old burial yard at the edge of town. Planks from shattered coffins littered the floor.

Bits of skeletons lay about. Only one casket remained intact. The black-cloaked figure inside was as still as death—until its yellow eyes fluttered open.

"What is it?" one man screamed, his voice filled with horror.

"Burn it! That thing is not human. Set it on fire!" another said as he threw his coal oil lantern on the body.

"Feed the fire. Throw the boards from the other coffins onto the flames," Warren ordered.

Panic made the men clumsy, but they managed to stoke the fire, and angry flames licked the air.

The fire burned until morning while the men stood guard for fear of the flames spreading. But their vigilance wasn't needed. Only that one small area, a room that had once been a burial vault, burned. By morning, smouldering ashes were all that remained of the evil. Finally the town was safe from the unnatural predator.

Or so the people thought.

Some 20 years later on a fine summer's evening, a young woman looking out her bedroom window could have sworn she had seen something moving in the distance. She looked again and it was gone. *Probably just a piece of black cloth blown up against the fence,* she thought, and went back to reading her book—one of the horror stories she loved to read.

Hidden Treasure

Jennifer could hardly believe her luck, a house for sale in *that* area. Her heart soared as she read the newspaper advertisement and recognized the address. She could be living in the same neighbourhood as the Prime Minister of Canada. What a great real estate investment that would be—like finding hidden treasure. Jennifer knew she had to act quickly.

She closed her office door. Company regulations were clear. There were to be no personal calls during business hours, and even though she owned the company, Jennifer usually followed the rules. Today's call was going to have to be an exception. She had always wanted to live in that area of Ottawa. Plus, she was curious about the last sentence in the ad. It read, "If you're the lucky person to buy this house, I'll tell you about the home's most unique feature."

Smiling in anticipation, she picked up the phone. The man who answered confirmed everything he had specified in the newspaper. "The best thing for you to do is drive past the house. If you like what you see then just ring the bell and I'll show you around," he told her.

"I can be there in an hour," she replied, knowing that appearing so anxious wasn't going to help her bargaining position if she did decide to bid on the house.

Forty minutes later, Jennifer parked her car in front of the address the man had given her—and gasped. "I'm in love," she whispered to herself. "Elegant" was the only word she could think of to describe the century-old, two-storey brick house. A wide walkway led to stone steps and a screened-in veranda. When she got to the front door, she looked back across the front lawn. The grounds were equally gorgeous. Jennifer had found her dream home.

She was about to ring the bell when a middle-aged man opened the ornately carved oak door. "You must be Jennifer. I'm Richard. Please come in."

The young woman stepped into the front hall and then stopped dead in her tracks. What was she thinking? What kind of a stupid, dangerous thing was she doing? She was alone in a house with a complete stranger, and no one— except he and she—even knew she was there.

"We'll both feel more comfortable, I'm sure, if I just leave this front door open while you're here," the man said as if reading her mind.

Jennifer relaxed and brought the conversation back to real estate. "It's not often that a house on this street comes up for sale."

There wasn't any need for either of them to comment any further on the cachet of living in that neighbourhood.

"I'll show you through the house now, shall I?"

Twenty minutes later the pair was back in the front hall. Jennifer had liked each room more than the last. It had been a very long time since she'd felt this happy, and trying to hide her positive emotions was hopeless.

"Richard, I'll tell you flat out, I want to buy the house. You're asking a fair price, especially considering the location, but you do need to tell me what the 'unique feature' is that you mentioned in the ad."

The man spoke quietly. "You do seem serious about buying the place, so yes, we should talk for a moment.

There's really no gentle way to word this. The house is haunted."

"I see." Jennifer's tone of voice contradicted her words. She didn't, in fact, "see" at all but simply needed to stall for time while the news sunk in.

"The phantom is completely harmless, and to be honest with you, I've actually become quite fond of him over the years."

"I see," she repeated in the same confused-sounding tone.

"He's quite the character, this ghost—a real creature of habit to be sure. Every night, no matter what time I go to bed, five minutes later he walks through my bedroom."

Jennifer nodded mutely while her mind raced, trying to figure out if Richard was joking or if he was a raving lunatic. At least the front door was open.

"I guess the word 'walk' doesn't really describe the way the ghost moves. 'Glide' would be a better word. He comes through the wall on the west side of the bedroom, then glides across the floor until he gets to about the middle of the room, just in front of my chest of drawers. Then he stops and points at the wall."

Richard looked at Jennifer as if he expected her to say something. When it was clear that she wasn't going to, he continued. "After that, the image simply vanishes. And that's the whole story. It's not much of a haunting, really, but I would be remiss if I let you buy the house without telling you about his presence."

Jennifer gulped and nodded. She was speechless.

The man continued calmly, "I have no idea who the fellow is, but it's easy to tell he's a ghost because you can see right through him. Then after he's pointed at the wall, his image just dissolves into crystals and he disappears."

Jennifer's voice was shaky. "Well, I guess your choice of words in the newspaper ad was sure accurate. A haunting definitely qualifies as a 'unique feature' in any home. I really don't know what to say. Do you have any idea why the ghost is here or why he always points at the wall?"

"None. I did a lot of redecorating when I moved in. It looked as though there'd been a big picture covering exactly where the ghost points, but it didn't matter to me because I had to paint the whole room anyway," he said before asking, "You're not afraid of ghosts, are you?"

Jennifer paused. "I suppose I've never thought about it one way or the other. This one doesn't sound like he's anything to be afraid of."

"You're right. I've enjoyed him. There are so few things in life that you can absolutely depend on, but that ghost walking through my bedroom exactly five minutes after I get into bed every night has certainly become something I count on. I'll probably miss him for a while after I move, but I've been offered a terrific promotion in the company's Kingston office and I'm not about to turn it down because I might get lonely for a ghost!"

"Okay," Jennifer said. "Haunted or not, I want to buy this house and I'm prepared to offer you the full asking price."

The two shook hands, and by the time she'd moved into the house a few weeks later, with its great location and gorgeous garden, she'd pushed any thoughts about the "unique feature" well to the back of her mind.

Just after midnight on moving day, Jennifer decided she'd done all the work she could for that day. Thanking her foresight in packing fresh towels and bed linen in a suitcase so she wouldn't have to hunt through boxes to find them, the woman contentedly climbed into bed for the first time in her dream home.

A few minutes later, something made her open her eyes. Unfamiliar house noises maybe? Or wait, did something move? There *was* a movement, over by the wall. She bolted upright, her eyes as big as saucers. It was the ghost! She could see him clearly, yet she could also see right through him.

It occurred to her that she should probably be frightened, but she wasn't even startled because this was so obviously the ghost that Richard had told her about. As Jennifer watched in fascination, the phantom stopped about halfway across the room and pointed to the wall. Then, before she could as much as consider what she'd seen, the image simply dissolved before her eyes.

"Wait," she called. "Who are you? What do you want?" But it was too late. The ghost was gone.

Jennifer's heart was racing, not with fear but with excitement and curiosity. She couldn't even *think* of sleeping now. Her mind whirled at warp speed. She remembered that the movers had left her small toolbox on the kitchen floor. She'd need to repair that wall anyway because it was marked from Richard's furniture, so there was nothing to lose and the possibility of solving a supernatural mystery to gain. At most only a few hammer blows stood between her and the answer.

The first strike with the hammer barely dented the wall. At least she had proof that the house was solidly built. By the time she finally succeeded in crashing through the plaster, Jennifer had lost track of how many times she'd pounded the wall, but once she'd managed to knock a small hole through it, she twisted the end of the hammer around and used the claw to enlarge the hole.

A mound of plaster dust and debris lay at her feet as she traded the hammer for a flashlight. Its beam illuminated spider webs and dust that had lain undisturbed for decades. Disappointed, Jennifer concluded that she had done nothing but make a mess and waste her time and energy. She pulled the flashlight back out of the hole, but as she did, something caught her eye.

What was it? A wooden block? No, it wasn't. It was a shelf. Someone had built a shelf inside the wall, but the flashlight's beam wasn't strong enough to let her see it clearly. She picked up the hammer and used the claw end again to pull away the edges of the hole until it was just a bit larger.

She had been right—it was a shelf—but *what* was that on it? A shudder ran through Jennifer's body. Slowly she put the hammer down and picked up the flashlight again. The beam of light showed her a dirty old sack lying on the shelf.

Tentatively, she reached her arm into the hole and bent her wrist just enough to grasp the sack. The material was rough to the touch, probably canvas. Jennifer gripped it as firmly as she could. After all this trouble, she couldn't risk having the answer to the puzzle literally slip from her hand. She pulled the sack safely through hole in the wall, but doing so caused a cloud of dust to billow up around her. Jennifer sneezed violently and dropped the bag at her feet, spilling its contents.

There, lying on the chunks of plaster and layers of dust, were dozens and dozens of hundred-dollar bills—hidden treasure.

The Death of You

The first streaks of sunrise angled through his bedroom window. Brad sat on the edge of the bed rubbing his whiskered jaw. A half-empty bottle of scotch stood on the nightstand beside him, but even so he hadn't slept, hadn't as much as laid his head on the pillow. For days now, grief had been his only emotion—until a long-buried memory from the year before triggered the addition of guilt and remorse.

It had been one of those perfect summer evenings. He had hit the bar after work like he usually did, but unlike most other days, he hadn't stayed until he couldn't walk straight—because he'd met a woman. By now he had no recollection of her name or even if he'd known it then. It didn't matter. He would never see her again. What had mattered at the time was that she seemed to like him. Funny, he couldn't recall if she held any appeal for him. Like her name, that hadn't been important. It was enough that she had been interested in him.

They had left the bar together, laughing and chatting. By the time they had wound their way to the path by the Chatham riverside they were holding hands. Brad had been delighted when he recognized his roommate Norm coming toward them, running with his beloved dog, Ruff. Great animal, that one—smart as a whip, and Norm had him so well trained. It made Brad wonder if he should get a pet himself. The house they lived in was big enough for two dogs, and going for a run looked like it might be a better way to ease away the workday's tensions than sitting through happy hour at the tavern. Of course, then he wouldn't be holding hands with a woman and getting ready to show her off.

"Hey, buddy!" Brad called to the approaching figure. His voice sounded louder and harsher than he'd expected it to.

"Oh, hi. Sorry, didn't see you," Norm jogged on the spot and gave his dog the hand command to sit.

"We're out for a walk," Brad explained, indicating his hand clasping the woman's.

Ruff growled, and when Norm moved the palm of his right hand to where the dog could see the command for silence, he whimpered and shifted nervously on his haunches, his ears flattened against his head.

"Sorry. He's usually friendly," Norm said, hoping that the sound of his voice would soothe the German shepherd.

The dog's lip curled up threateningly, and his growl reverberated from deep in its throat.

The woman stared at Ruff and then looked up at Norm. "That dog is going to be the death of you," she said.

Brad and Norm exchanged uncomfortable looks, both desperately wishing the encounter had never begun or, at the very least, that one of them would find a way to end it as soon as possible.

"I'd better be on my way," Norm said, laying his hand on Ruff's side.

Brad expelled a breath he hadn't known he'd been holding. "Yeah, okay. Maybe we should get that lawn cut this evening."

"Sure," Norm said, suspicious that Brad's comment had a lot more to do with wanting to lose the woman he'd picked up than it did with the length of the grass surrounding the house they rented. Brad really did attract bizarre types. Why would anyone have said something like that about the dog being the death of him?

Much to Brad's relief, Norm never asked about the woman from the bar. If he noticed that Brad had cut back on his drinking he didn't mentioned that either, and life went on as it had before the awkward incident had ever occurred.

One rainy spring day, Brad came home from work and found the house empty. *Only a truly dedicated pet owner would think of exercising his dog in this weather,* Brad thought as he poured himself a glass of cola and sat on the porch watching the rain pour down.

It wasn't long before Norm, with Ruff trailing, came around the corner, both of them drenched to the bone. Laughing, Brad got up to throw an old beach towel down on the front hall floor. That's when he heard the thud of a car hitting something—something made of flesh and bones.

"Norm!" he screamed, and ran for the door.

Norm had crumpled onto the road beside the lifeless body of his beloved dog. When Brad tried to help him, the grief-stricken man screamed at him to go away. Sobbing, Norm carried the animal's limp carcass to the woods behind the backyard, determined to dig the grave himself.

Partly out of respect for the man's need to be alone in his mourning, but mostly because he needed a drink, Brad made his way to the tavern.

Brad found Norm's body lying in the mud beside Ruff's. The coroner reasoned that Norm's digging disturbed a rattler that had burrowed for protection from the deluge. The snake had plunged its fangs into the man's arm and released its deadly venom.

Brad could barely comprehend the awful irony of what had happened. Norm had died burying his beloved dog. He shuddered as he remembered the awkward incident in the park that had occurred nearly a year ago. Who could that woman have been?

"That dog will be the death of you."

Brad reached for the bottle.

Chapter 4: Last Quarter

A Morning Walk

Grant opened his eyes slowly and looked around the darkened room. What could have wakened him? He had been having a dream, that much he knew for certain, because he still had a clear image of himself standing in a barren corridor and being unsure which one of two doors he was supposed to pull open.

What time was it? Still the middle of the night? Maybe not, but certainly not dawn yet. He hadn't had enough sleep, that was for sure, especially considering the day he had ahead of him. It was his last day at the lake, his beloved Canoe Lake. He'd been staying at his uncle's cottage for more than a week now, since the July 1st weekend. His older brother and sisters had left for their jobs in the city a couple of days ago. Grant had stayed on not just because his summer obligations hadn't started yet but also because this time, leaving the lake symbolized leaving any pretense of childhood behind him. He had a decision to make—effectively which one of the two dream-doors to open—but either way, the adventures and responsibilities of adulthood were directly ahead. He lay back down on the pillow with his hands behind his head, staring at the ceiling and smiling with anticipation.

Nearby an owl offered its distinctive hoot, a sound Grant took as an invitation to get outside and enjoy this last morning at the lake. He pulled on a pair of shorts and let the screen door slam closed behind him. The sky was overcast, and raindrops bounced off the calm surface of the lake. Grant breathed deeply. He loved that smell.

It was as if the water-washed air had been freshly made just for him to enjoy as he strolled near the shore, lost in the satisfaction of feeling absolutely alone in the familiar and beautiful surroundings.

When a movement in the woods caught his eye he wondered, just for a moment, if there might be a bear roaming in the area, but then as he looked to his right he could see a flash of white canvas—a tent. It was just a camper he had seen moving.

Grant stayed on the path, wanting to walk past unnoticed so as not to disturb his sense of peaceful isolation. And he might have succeeded if he hadn't stepped on large twig. The snap reverberated in the early morning silence, and a man called out, "Hello?"

"Sorry," Grant called out. "I didn't mean to bother you."

"No bother at all," the tall, thin man said, brushing a lock of black hair from his forehead. "I was just fixing breakfast. Would you care to join me?"

Grant smiled. Why couldn't social interaction be this friendly and open in the city? "I'd like that. Thank you," he replied, making his way to the man's campsite.

The two hunkered down over tin plates filled with fried bacon and bread. They ate in a companionable silence, and when they were done Grant thanked his host for the delicious meal, adding, "I'm staying at my uncle's cottage just back there a bit. My name is Grant."

The man nodded. "I know who you are. I've been around here for a lot of years. My name is Tom. If you don't have to run off right away, I could put a pot of coffee over the fire."

Grant thought for a moment; it probably wasn't even six o'clock yet, and a cup of fresh, strong coffee made over an open fire always tasted especially good by the lake. "I'd like that, Tom," the young man said. "Anything I can do to help?"

"Yeah, you could get me a spoon out of the cutlery tray in the tent," Tom suggested.

Grant pulled back the tent flap, stepped inside and stood stock-still. The small canvas structure was filled with paintings—oil paintings of all sizes and shapes. They were stark and dramatic. Grant didn't pride himself on knowing much about art, but these were impressive even to his untrained eye. For some reason the paintings looked somehow familiar. He picked up the spoon and went back outside.

Once the coffee in the scarred old metal pot was bubbling into the lid's glass dome, Tom used a tree branch and, with a practiced hand, lifted the pot from the fire. The aroma was tantalizing, and the taste of the brew lived up to that promise. It was the best cup of coffee Grant had ever sipped: piping hot and strong.

The pair emptied their mugs in silence. Then Grant thanked the man again and said, "Those paintings in your tent are magnificent. Are they your work?"

"They are. Do you like them?" Tom asked.

Grant nodded.

"Take one. Choose the one you like best and take it. My gift to you."

"I couldn't, not without paying you for it, and I could never afford what they must sell for."

Tom stood and walked into the tent. A moment later he handed Grant a small piece of board. It was clearly a painting of Canoe Lake from this exact vantage point. "Give it to your mother, Grant. I think she'd like this one. Now off you go. We both have other places we need to be."

Grant walked back to the cottage holding the painting, pleased because he knew his mother would indeed be tickled by the gift. He laid the painting on the backseat of the car. Then he threw his clothes into a suitcase and, with an enormous sense of nostalgia for all he was leaving behind, began the drive south.

As he neared the city, he turned on the car radio. CBC was doing a retrospective on the Canadian artists known as the Group of Seven. The announcer introduced a guest to be interviewed: an authority on art history. The expert acknowledged the introduction and added, "It's quite a coincidence that we should be talking about this today. July 8th is the anniversary of Tom Thomson's death at Canoe Lake in 1917. There's an old legend that his ghost appears at the lake every year on this date."

Grant felt like he had been punched in the stomach. He pulled over to the side of the road and slowed the car to a stop. Now he realized why the paintings had looked familiar. Had he eaten breakfast with a ghost? Not possible. Besides, the man had given him a painting. It was right there in the backseat.

But it wasn't. Dried-out woodchips lay scattered across the backseat of the car. Some of them had flecks of colour peeling from them.

Her Picture

"This is a mansion, Arlene. Why didn't you tell me?" Jane asked as she put her suitcase down on the marble floor of the foyer in her friend's home in Whitby.

"Come in, come in," Arlene replied, extending her arm in welcome. "I'll explain it all to you once we're settled at the dinner table."

Less than an hour later, the two women were sitting at a small table overlooking a tailored garden. Arlene offered a toast to her friend's visit and then, as she always had to when people visited for the first time, began to explain why she lived in such a grand old house.

"My family came from Britain in the middle of the 19th century. Those were boom years in southern Ontario, and my ancestors were hardworking people whose goal was to acquire land. They worked the real estate market well and became wealthy quite quickly," Arlene explained.

"So I can see," Jane said between mouthfuls of a delicious seafood lasagna.

"This was the grandest of their homes. My great-great-uncle built this place, and it's been in the family ever since. My father found the commute a bit much because he worked in downtown Toronto, but with technology and my career, driving to an office isn't even an issue. No one in the family has ever wanted to sell this house; it's effectively our ancestral home, and I've been designated as its caretaker for this generation."

"What a story, and thanks for inviting me to spend the weekend. It's wonderful to see you again after so long, and getting away from routine is just good for a person's soul, I always think…but I never anticipated staying in a castle," Jane said, looking around for a second and third time.

Arlene chuckled dismissively. "Tomorrow we'll go for a drive around town; I'll show you what a real castle looks like."

The two friends spent a pleasant evening by the fireplace catching up on each other's lives since they had last seen one another in college. When Arlene noticed Jane stifling a yawn, she suggested that they call it a night. "I've put your suitcase in the front bedroom on the third floor, if that's all right. It's like a tower up there. You'll like the view, I'm sure. It's actually one of the nicest rooms in the house, but it's not used very often—I've never been sure why."

Arlene was right. It *was* a nice room, and Jane felt very much at home. She was asleep before she knew it. Sometime later, she woke up. For a moment she lay still, keeping her eyes closed and wondering what had disturbed her sleep. The house was quiet, but something felt odd. Jane sat up and looked around.

A harsh orange light poured in from the front window. *Just moonlight*, she thought as she pulled the blankets up around her shoulders. And that's when she saw the ethereal figure of a woman in a long, white dress, looking out the window and clutching a bundle to her chest. Her image oozed evil. Terror spread through Jane's veins as she watched the woman hurl the bundle out the window.

Jane tried to scream but couldn't make a sound. The woman's transparent image turned from the window and glared at Jane, who couldn't help committing to memory the spectre's striking features. She must have been a beauty, but now her dark eyes flashed with hatred and her mouth was pursed in a triumphant smirk. The air in the room went stale and sour. As Jane watched in fascinated horror, the image grew faint and then vaporized completely.

The next morning she decided not to say anything to her host about the terrifying spectacle she'd witnessed in the middle of the night. She didn't want her friend to think she was unappreciative of the hospitality—nor did she want to even think about the incident, much less describe it in words. Instead she tried to convince herself that she hadn't really wakened in the middle of the night, that it had all simply been a nightmare caused by her unfamiliar surroundings.

Jane and Arlene spent the day driving around the town and then hiking in the woods at the outskirts. In the evening they sat in large, well-padded leather chairs reading and warming themselves by an enormous fireplace.

As they turned in for the night, Jane thanked her host again and added, "I feel as though I'm a lady in some grand English estate."

"I'm glad you're enjoying your visit. It's wonderful to have you here," Arlene replied.

This time Jane was just climbing into bed when the odd light flooded the room again. She watched in horror as the scene from the night before played itself out before her eyes. The same transparent figure stood at the window clasping something to her chest. A stench of evil permeated the air in the room as the spectre once again threw the bundle out the window and then turned to stare at Jane.

Rivulets of cold sweat ran down her body, and she shook with convulsive shudders. After a time the air in the room began to freshen, and slowly she was able to unfold her limbs. This frightening scene hadn't been a dream. Something terrible had happened here, something so terrible that it had permanently scarred the psychic tone in this room.

Too afraid to run for help but equally afraid of staying in the obviously haunted room, Jane knew she had to clear her head of the image. She remembered packing notepaper into her suitcase. She wondered if she could draw the phantom's image; if she could, then perhaps getting it on paper would help to get the vile face out of her mind. The sketch turned out to be a good likeness, but instead of freeing her from the memory of the apparition, the drawing reinforced its impact on her mind. Jane lay shivering and fully awake until sunrise.

At breakfast, Jane made an excuse as to why she was so tired and told her friend that despite the original plan to stay another day, she would have to be on her way shortly. Arlene was clearly disappointed, so Jane asked her to accompany her up to the third-floor room to chat while she packed to leave. On the way upstairs, in order to break the tension between them, Jane made a point to ask about the old-fashioned, formal portraits that lined the walls of the staircase.

One by one Arlene identified each of her ancestors. "There's only one person who's ever lived here whose portrait isn't hanging in this house. It's hidden away in the attic," Arlene added.

"Every family has a black sheep, I guess," Jane replied, trying to keep the conversation light.

Arlene stood quietly as Jane slowly packed her clothes and contemplated whether or not she should mention the terrifying incidents she had experienced on the previous two nights. As she picked up her book from the nightstand she uncovered the sketch she had made of the ghost's cruel face.

Arlene gasped. "Where did you find this drawing?"

"I didn't find it," Jane said a bit defensively. "I sketched the face last night. I didn't want to tell you, but this face is why I'm anxious to leave. Your house, well this bedroom anyway, is haunted. I know it is because I've seen the ghost. That's how I was able to draw her picture."

Arlene sat down heavily on a chair beside the bed. It was fully a minute before she was able to speak. "The woman you've drawn was my great-great-uncle's second wife. It's her portrait that's hidden away in the attic. My uncle's first wife died in childbirth, leaving a newborn daughter. His second wife was hideously jealous of his relationship with the baby. One day my uncle found his daughter's crumpled body on the stone walkway beside the house. His wife lived the rest of her life under a cloud of suspicion, but nothing could ever be proven."

It was clear to Jane that the tragedy was as distressing to Arlene as it had been to the generations that had gone before. Should she tell her friend what she had seen or not? Keeping this secret could be damaging to them both.

Jane decided to be honest. "There might not have been any proof before, but there certainly is now. This room is haunted. It's as if that woman's murderous deed is being played over and over again on a continuous loop in this room's atmosphere. I saw her apparition—twice. She threw something from the window and then turned around and stared at me."

The two women stared at one another. There was nothing left to say.

A Daughter's Devotion

It was nearly midnight. The streets of Kingston glistened with rain, but the downpour had eased now and all was still—save a small shape rounding the corner, furtively scurrying from building to building.

Dr. Randall sat in his dimly lit study smoking his pipe. He looked 20 years older than he was. The year was 1919. The Great War had finally given up its slaughter, only to be replaced by carnage from the Spanish flu. Randall had practiced medicine in this small community for his entire career, and until recently it had been a rewarding calling. Lately, though, he was feeling frustrated and discouraged.

He banged his fist on the padded arm of his leather chair. How could he win the battle to save lives when he didn't know what he was fighting? What was the point of trying? What was the point of life itself? It all seemed so futile.

When Randall heard the first knock at the door he ignored it, sure that the sound was only a figment of his badly troubled mind. But then it came again.

"Who could be at my door at this time of night?" he grumbled to himself as he made his way to the front hallway. He pulled open the door and a gust of cold air swirled around him. For an instant he thought the sounds *had* been his imagination because there was no one at his door. Then he looked down. There stood a small child, a girl, huddled in a ripped coat, drenched with rain, her hair plastered to her head.

Without a word, the waif grasped his hand and pulled him out of the house and into the street. Every few steps she looked back at the doctor, urging him to keep following. She led him down an alley and between buildings to an open doorway. There, on a cot in the corner, lay a woman's body.

Randall realized that the child must somehow have known where he lived and thought that, perhaps, he could help. But was the woman dead? He felt for a pulse. It was weak, but at least she was still alive. He felt her forehead. She was burning up with fever, but still she was lucid enough to respond to his touch with a sigh.

The man scrubbed his hands and looked around the shabby room. There was a hot plate—he could make some broth to comfort her, but that was about all he could offer. Perhaps he could make enough to give both the woman and her child some comfort.

When the broth was heated, Randall cradled the woman's head carefully and lifted her to something close to a sitting position. She opened her almost lifeless eyes when he spooned warm broth into her mouth. Soon the dullness left the woman's eyes. He set the cup and spoon down and went to get a cloth to wipe her chin. As he did, he saw the coat—the ragged coat that the child had been wearing when she had come to his door an hour before. It was the same coat, he knew that for certain—there was the torn sleeve. But this coat was warm and dry. How could that be? Less than an hour ago, when the girl was wearing it, it had been soaking wet.

Randall looked around. When he saw that the woman was managing to drink from the cup by herself, he picked up the coat and held it out to her. "Whose coat is this?" he asked.

The woman's voice was small and weak. "It was my daughter's. I haven't had the heart to force myself to part with it. She died last month—the flu took her."

It was nearly dawn. All was quiet. The streets of Kingston were still glistening with rain, but once the sun came up they would be dry in no time, and the hustle and bustle of the day would begin.

Dr. Randall sat in his dimly lit study smoking his pipe. He was tired and confused to the very depth of his being, but the frustration and discouragement that had been evident on his face only hours before was gone. He drummed his fingers on the padded arm of his leather chair. How could he explain to anyone, even to himself, what had happened that night? What was the point of trying? Perhaps there was a point to life. Perhaps it wasn't all so futile after all.

Fate

"What are you talking about? You can't leave work and go home! The store has only been open for a couple of hours. You've just come back from getting yourself a cup of coffee for goodness sakes. You can't tell me you're sick all of a sudden. You were fine a few minutes ago." The store manager made no attempt to hide his aggravation. It was Saturday, the most profitable day of the week, and this was the busiest store in London. He needed a full complement of staff today of all days.

"Please, let me go home, Ray. I'll be back tomorrow morning. I promise," Trisha replied quietly.

The man paused before answering. "Now that I get a closer look at you, I have to admit that you're as white as a sheet. What the heck's going on? Everything was fine half an hour ago when you and Candace took off for break."

Trisha sighed. "I suppose I owe you the truth. When we went into the food court to get coffee, Fate was standing there staring at me. She shot me the weirdest look. It scared the life out of me."

"Faye? Faye who? What are you talking about?"

"No. Not Faye. Fate."

"You saw Fate. That's a good one; it isn't even April Fool's Day or anything. Ha ha ha." His voice was dripping with ridicule. He paused, and when he spoke again it was clear that any concern he might have had for the young woman's well being was gone. "Yeah, I think you *had* better go home for the rest of the day. And drop in to get a doctor's note before you bother coming back."

Shaking his head, he watched as his usually reliable employee turned and left the store with her shoulders hunched and her arms wrapped tightly around her body.

"Candace!" Ray barked. "Trish has gone home. She's also gone crazy. What the heck happened out in that food court?"

"I'm not sure. She said a woman was staring at her, and right after that, man, she just couldn't get out of there fast enough."

Ray shook his head. "I'm going to check it out. If there's a weirdo out there we should call security."

Weaving through metal tables and chairs, trying not to breathe in the greasy-smelling air, the irritated man scanned the food court. Nothing looked odd. Humiliation burned his gut. He'd been duped. As he turned back toward his store, he stopped. Now to add to his foul humour, he had the unpleasant impression that he was being watched.

He looked around. He was right. Someone *was* watching him—a woman, over in the corner, near the washrooms.

That's the oldest woman I've ever seen, Ray thought. *That must be the woman who freaked Trish out.* He called out to the crone, "Hello! Hello, ma'am! I need to talk to you. Do you realize that you scared one of my employees? I don't know who you are, but you stared at her and upset her so much that she left and went home. I have to tell you, I'm pretty annoyed. Because of you, my entire Saturday is totally messed up."

The elderly woman nodded before she spoke, and when she did speak her voice was surprisingly strong and her tone surprisingly aggressive. "Your day is not the only one that's messed up. And besides, I didn't mean to stare at her. Even Fate has manners, you know. I was just surprised to see her here. She and I have an appointment this morning. We're supposed to meet at her house in an hour."

Ray slumped against the cold tile wall. He watched as the old woman walked away. Her image blurred a bit before disappearing entirely.

Past Death Do Us Part

"For richer and for poorer, in sickness and in health, till death us do part" were the vows I'd taken in a tiny church near Sarnia, 28 years ago. And they were vows I'd kept until this morning, but then this morning I'd been released from my obligations.

It was ironic that my emancipator had turned out to be Julia. She wasn't a woman I had ever even considered in the role of saviour; she was an enemy and had been from that summer day in 1894, when she first laid eyes on my husband, Marcus.

The love between the two of them had been sickeningly obvious right from the start. Despite that, like a fool, I fought for years to retain both my dignity and my marriage. After a time, though, it became clearly and painfully evident even to me that Marcus and I were married in name only. He loved Julia but didn't have the courage to leave me or the security that I represented and that she, most assuredly, did not. From then on, I held my head high and acted as though their carry-on didn't exist.

Oh, I tried to remind him that he had only prospered with my support and that not all women would have been able, or willing, to have taken on as much as I had. It had always been me who had been sure to set aside a little something at the end of each year. My determination had paid off. After almost 30 years, we had accumulated a tidy sum—a very tidy sum actually, a sum 10 times greater than he knew. But none of that mattered anymore. Now all I needed to do was stand back and watch the unfortunate circumstances that they had created unfold.

It had been so quick. Quick and surprisingly painless. I was dead before I knew it. They had it well planned, that was certain. Julia had approached the front door with a hard, determined manner about her. I'd thought she was coming to confront me, but just seconds after I saw her come up the path to the house, everything went black.

Using her supposed visit as a distraction, Marcus had placed himself directly behind me, his gun at the base of my skull—pointing up just slightly.

As I floated away, I watched the two of them working, almost in unison and at a fevered pace. It was clear from their determined moves that they had rehearsed this, at least in their minds, many times. Covered in my blood from his head to his shoes, my husband reached toward the grandfather clock that had stood in our living room since the day we were married. At the same time as he was pulling it down, he turned it around. The back of the enormous timepiece hit the carpeted floor with a thud.

Julia unlocked the pendulum case and threw open its glass door. She looked over at Marcus and when she saw that he was at the head of my bloodied corpse, she moved to my ankles. Together, they fought to cram my lifeless body into the clock. Then, one at each end, they laboured to carry their load outside to the wagon. I could feel my former self being bumped along the rough trail and wondered, vaguely, where they were headed with their incriminating load.

A clock as my coffin, I thought with an unexpected laugh. *How timely*.

Suddenly I wondered: I could hear them; did that mean they could hear me? If so, I'd better not be lying in here, deader than yesterday's catch, giggling at my own silly puns. Complete silence was becoming more and more difficult, for with each bump in the track I realized that we were heading for the lake. They intended to throw the clock, with my body as an anchor, into the deep, black water of the lake that, for so many years, had provided us with life-sustaining water.

I nearly laughed again when I realized that our nest egg, a collection of rare, slim, hand-written, centuries-old books, would be ruined, worthless, the moment the water surged around them. At the time that I'd ordered these precious volumes, I'd prided myself on my ingenuity. Marcus didn't know about my investment. Even if he had found them, he couldn't have spent that portion of our savings impulsively because the bills of sale were in my name, and also, re-sale would have to be arranged through a broker. Marcus wouldn't know the first thing about that process.

None of that mattered now anyway. I was dead and the lovers had what they thought they wanted. My collection of fine books lay underneath the panel of wood that Marcus had always thought was simply the back of the clock.

I could feel my eternal time capsule being transferred from the wagon to the boat. "Just keep your grip a moment longer," I could hear Marcus order in a strained voice.

The couple's grunts of exertion were followed by the jolt of my coffin being lowered onto the bottom of our rowboat. A slapping, thumping sound and then the cold, dark water closed in around me. Slowly at first, and then with a little more speed, my entombed body sank until it came to a stop in the silt at the bottom of the lake. After only a few seconds of shifting and settling, all was still.

Again, I wanted to laugh—this time wryly. I doubted that either Marcus or Julia could hear me now, but even so I was relieved when I regained my self-control. I knew they'd be rowing for shore by now. I also knew that the ink would have run off all the pages of my ancient, hand-written investments. They would be blank and soggy now, utterly worthless. I bided my time happily because time was something I had a great deal of. I was at rest, in complete darkness and silence. Why, from here I could even have gone directly to my final reward. But first I had a little unfinished business to attend to.

I reached underneath me and pried up a corner of the false backing that had hidden my investments so well for so many years. Barely able to reach even one book, I suddenly realized that it didn't matter a whit if I didn't happen to get a firm hold on a volume. All I needed was to be able to grasp a few pages from any one of them.

Once I had half a dozen pieces of paper clutched in my hands, I waited until I guessed it was close to midnight. Then, careful not to lose my grasp on the sheets, I let my ethereal self float to the surface of the lake and then to the shore by my house. Well, the house that had been mine.

I opened the front door quietly. Marcus and Julia were asleep in the bed that Marcus and I had shared for nearly three decades. Both were snoring heavily. If either of their consciences were troubling them, the exhaustion from their labours had overridden any guilt-provoked insomnia that might have momentarily plagued either of them.

I didn't disturb the sleeping couple but just walked to the kitchen and laid a still-wet book cover and a few ink-stained leaves of parchment on the kitchen table. The gold-engraved lettering on the cover's spine would provide a clue as to what the soaked, illegible pages once contained. Satisfied, I left again by the front door. As I turned back to take one last look into the home that had been mine for all of my marriage, I noticed that I'd left wet, muddy footprints across the floor—from the door to the bedroom, then into the kitchen, and then back to the door. Feeling entirely satisfied, I let that door close with a bang of finality.

The thought crossed my mind briefly that staying on this earthly plane even a few more hours would give me the opportunity to witness my murderers' reactions to my gifts from beyond the grave, but even that delicious thought wasn't tempting enough for me to postpone my journey.

I was ready to meet my maker. My scores were evened.

Love Paid the Debt

Living on the outskirts of Kenora during the Dirty Thirties was no one's idea of luxury, but George and Amelia Davidson knew they were more fortunate than most. In addition to their good health, they had the security of knowing that they loved one other dearly and had for decades. That comfort meant the world to them.

Together they made an industrious and determined team who had worked diligently to pay down the mortgage they owed on their small farm. The last payment was due December 1st, just a few weeks away. Once the loan had been paid in full, the farm, the house and all the other buildings on the property would be theirs. They would be as financially secure as any couple could be in such a desolate era.

"It's going to be a happy day when we clear that debt," Amelia said, hugging George as he got ready to go into town.

George whistled as he hooked the horses up to the hay wagon and headed out to sell the last of the crop he and Amelia had harvested. It would be a long, slow ride along rutted dirt roads, but he didn't mind. He'd have walked the route, pulling the cart himself if he'd had to, because the money he made selling the load would cover the final mortgage payment. They would be debt free forever.

Amelia set about cleaning the house and doing the laundry. Before she knew it, the sun had gone down; the day was over. She glanced out the window to see if she could see George driving the team back through the gate, but there was no sign of him yet. *He'll be home soon*, she told herself as she sat down in the easy chair by the fire. Soon she was contentedly asleep.

Several hours later, Amelia woke up feeling disoriented. Taking a nap was not something she did very often. How long had she slept? What time was it? Where was George?

Amelia stumbled to the kitchen. The clock's hands read 9:00 PM. This wasn't good. She knew that George would never have stayed away this long unless something had happened. The only thing she didn't know was how bad that something had been.

All night long the woman paced the house, sick with worry. At the first light of morning she bundled herself in jacket and gloves and boots and made her way into the farmyard. George *had* made it home after all. He must have been putting the horses away for the night when one of them kicked him. His skull was crushed. Amelia collapsed in a faint beside her husband's body, and an hour later, that's where a neighbour found them.

The woman was beyond consolation. Not only had she lost her beloved George, but now she could lose the farm as well because she had no idea where he kept their savings hidden. She would be destitute.

Word of the tragedy spread, and neighbours from near and far gathered around the distraught woman. Together they searched the property for George's hiding place for the money that would be due at the bank in just a few weeks. One person went through every piece of George's clothing while others scoured the house and outbuildings. Someone even sifted through the feed bins in the barn. No one could find the money.

Finally one of the George's closest friends offered to talk to the bank manager on Amelia's behalf. Surely he wouldn't take the farm away from a widow when there was only a few hundred dollars left owing on it. But this was the Depression, and the banker had heard it all before. He claimed that there was nothing he could do.

On the way back from the bank, that neighbour stopped in to the doctor's house and asked him to call on the distraught woman. If no one was going to be able to save the farm then someone at least needed to save Amelia. She hadn't slept for days.

"Take these, my dear," the doctor said as he handed two small tablets to the grieving widow. "They'll help you sleep."

And they did. Amelia was unconscious in no time and happily dreaming that she and George were still together. In her dream, George came to the door and beckoned to her. Deep snow covered the ground. He picked her up as if she were a small child and carried her to the back of the building where the tools were stored. Then he pointed up to a rafter. There, tucked into the corner almost out of sight, was a small jar—a small jar full of money.

As Amelia stirred toward consciousness, she whimpered, not wanting to leave George even if it was only in a dream. As she came fully awake, she became convinced that her dream was no ordinary dream; had George's ghost come to show her where he'd hidden the money? Amelia jumped to her feet and ran to the door. The farmyard was covered in freshly fallen snow. She pulled her heavy, wool coat off the hook near the door and wrapped it around herself before slipping her feet into lined boots and stepping outside.

Sharp crystals of snow stung her checks as she trekked through the knee-deep snow, across the yard, past the barn and on to the small building George had taken Amelia to in her dream. She dug away the snow that had drifted up against the door until she was finally able to pry it open.

There was the jar full of money! It was right where George's spirit had showed her it would be: on a rafter, tucked into a corner. Even after death, Amelia's beloved George had continued to look after her. The farm would be hers, free and clear.

The Pilot's Life

"Harv, hi there! I didn't expect to see you at Buttonville this morning. It's nearly 9:00. Shouldn't you be at the Island Airport by now?" Carol asked from her desk at the side of the pilots' lounge. "What brings you here?"

"Forgot my gloves. Got 'em now. Gotta run," the man replied.

"Well, have a good flight. See you back here at suppertime. I'll make sure the cook does up that corned beef you like so much." Carol smiled. She'd never have admitted it, but she was sweet on that pilot. She knew that she'd better go and talk to the cook right now because once she started concentrating on the paperwork that covered her desk, she might forget.

Carol hurried toward the cafeteria, hoping that the cook would be in a co-operative mood and that she hadn't left her request for the special order too late. As she hurried down the hall, the tantalizing aroma of spicy meat teased her nostrils. "Ralph," she called out to a man standing behind a serving counter. "I can't believe it. It smells like you're cooking corned beef!"

The man lowered his eyes. "I just started a minute ago when I heard the news. It seemed the best way to honour Harvey's memory."

"Harvey's memory?"

"Haven't you heard? It just happened. No one knows what caused it, but his plane exploded. He was barely off the ground at the island. I guess we can be thankful that it was so sudden. He must have died instantly."

Carol grasped the back of a cafeteria chair as the man continued to talk.

"He left his gloves here yesterday. I'm going to put them in a glass case by the door."

Tales from the Canadian Crypt

"Next time you offer someone a ride, at least make sure you have enough gas in your car to make the trip."

Rick didn't reply. He stared straight ahead through the windshield. An hour ago when they'd left the comic book convention, a creeping twilight had begun to bruise the sky. By now that moment seemed like a lifetime ago. The sky was fully dark, and the last familiar road sign he'd seen had been a good way back. Worse, it had been pointing to Bracebridge—not the direction they should've been headed in.

When the club president had asked Rick to drive the keynote speaker, none other than Will Arnold, to the airport, he felt so honoured that he could almost taste the happiness and pride surging through him. Now, 90 minutes later, dread and anxiety tasted sour in his throat. He and his passenger, his responsibility, none other than Will Arnold, were in serious trouble.

"Look at that gas gauge," Will continued, jabbing his finger toward the car's dashboard. "We're driving on nothing but fumes. There's a driveway up ahead. Turn in there. It's gotta lead to a house. Maybe someone there can help us."

The spot Will Arnold pointed to probably had been a driveway years before, but now it was barely a trail. Rick manoeuvred he car between two rows of dead and dying trees. His body gave a small, involuntary shudder. He was cold and frightened. As the path angled slightly to the right, the car's headlights flashed across a small wooden house.

"Go and check the place out," Arnold's order broke the darkened silence. "See if you can find some gas to siphon."

Rick expelled the breath he hadn't known he'd been holding. "I'm not going to steal. We're already trespassing. Besides, there's no car in the yard. There's no sign of life here at all."

"You can't be serious, you little wimp. This place is just a shack, and it's obviously abandoned. It's not stealing if no one lives here anymore."

"Even so, it belongs to someone. Look, there's even a name on the door—M REHWON or something," Rick pointed out.

"Like we have a choice," the older man snapped. "In case you haven't noticed, we're completely lost and the car's nearly out of gas. I'd say our options are limited to checking this place out or nothing."

Rick didn't answer. He wanted to remind his passenger that the gas they'd started out with would have been more than enough if they hadn't burned through a quarter tank's worth by trying the great Will Arnold's suggestion of a short-cut.

"Well all right then, *we'll* check the place out," the man barked.

Bits of gravel crunched in complaint under their foot-steps and mist rose around their ankles as the two men walked tentatively toward the house. Bare windows on either side of the open door stared vacantly at them, and tentacles of fog snaked along the building's foundation.

The pair stepped into the solitary room. Moonbeams shed a cold blue glow, casting more shadows than light.

"No one's been here for years," Will declared with great assuredness as his eyes adjusted to the tomb-like darkness.

"Maybe so, but it isn't just a shack. It was definitely someone's home." Rick gestured toward the broken-down tables and chairs that, by now, only served to cast odd shadowy shapes around the single room.

Will Arnold, an eloquent and long-winded speaker just few hours earlier, could only muster something resembling a grunt.

"You all right?" Rick asked, inching his way across the rotting floorboards to get closer to the other man. Darkness crept with him. Will didn't answer, but Rick could hear his shallow, laboured breathing. All he needed was for the guy to faint, or worse, to have a heart attack. "Look, if it's all the same to you, I think we should go back to the car. This place has a vicious vibe to it, man. It feels like something doesn't want us in here."

Will cleared his throat as he'd done several times during his speech earlier that evening. "Don't be ridiculous," he snapped. "The place is empty. There's no one here to want us or not to want us. Check out back. We might get lucky and find a can of gas."

A blast of ice-cold air swept past them.

"What the...?" Fear closed Rick's throat before he could finish speaking.

"Duh, Einstein. That'd be a draft or something." Taunting Rick clearly eased the man's nervousness. "It's a dilapidated old building. What can you expect? No need to be screaming like a girl. Anyway, we're not getting anywhere in that beaten up old car of yours; we're stuck here until morning, I've missed my flight—you'll be paying for the next one, by the way—and in the meantime, I'm checking the place out. A freaky setting like this could come in handy for new comic script."

Bile rose in Rick's throat. He didn't know whether he was more afraid of whatever unseen presence he could sense in the house or of the way Will was acting. The man had suddenly put his stage persona back on like it was a biker's black leather jacket.

"Check it out, Dick—that's your name, right? Dick?"

"It's Rick actually."

"Whatever. Look at this. It's a scrapbook. Someone's been drafting a graphic novel. I can hardly believe my luck. It looks good, completely original. I wonder why they just left it?"

"Maybe *they* were smart enough to get out of here. Fast." Rick made an effort to control his voice as he inched back toward the door. "Come on."

"Yeah, sure, whatever you say, but I'm taking this book with me. It's seriously good stuff, and it's mine now." Will tucked the yellowing notebook under his arm. Its brittle pages crinkled in protest. "What a stroke of luck. I'm going to publish this. I'll make a fortune. It's brilliant."

"I don't think you should take something that's not yours —especially not from a haunted house. You're inviting some absolutely brutal karma."

"Like you know anything, Dick. You're the one who ran out of gas and got us here in the first place. But yeah, okay, we'll go sit in the car until morning. Might as well. Nothing better to do. Besides, I want to have a better look at this scrapbook. The artwork's good and it'll be easy to copy. Did you see the title? *Tales from the Canadian Crypt* —pretty inventive if you ask me."

"What was *that*?" Rick yelled whirling around to peer back into the room.

"Settle down, will you. No need to freak out. Yeesh."

"I heard something—voices. I can hear voices. There's a bunch of people talking—all at once—off in the distance." Rick grabbed the man's arm and tried to pull him to the door.

"I gotta tell ya, kid, I can't hear anyone talking except you, but all right—if you want to get out of here so badly, I've already said I'd go."

"The voices stopped." Rick's voice had a high and brittle tone to it as he tried not to run out of the house.

Once they were back in the car, Will looked at Rick for the first time since the evening had begun. "See," he said. "Everything's okay."

"That place is solid evil," Rick replied. "Those voices were threatening us."

"Threatening you, maybe, but nothing's threatening me. This book is a golden goose that's going to lay golden eggs for me in every province and territory of this country. The dude who did it has stories set all over Canada. There's one about a werewolf in a prairie grain elevator and another one about a vampire living in a lighthouse on the coast. Just excellent. People will eat these stories right up. I'm dying to see the story for Ontario. Probably some devil-in-disguise Bay Street suit who's really a vampire."

Another blast of wind, strong enough to shake the car this time, interrupted the demented man's enthusiasm.

Rick's heart slammed against his rib cage, but his voice was strong with conviction. "I'm getting as far away from here as the few drops of gas we have left will get us."

He cranked the steering wheel as hard as he could, turning the car toward the road. Only then did he risk one last look back in his mirror at the horrible old house. As he did, his stomach clenched with a terrifying realization. That wasn't a name over the door. It was a word—a word that was spelled backwards. That letter wasn't an M. It was an E that had toppled over 90 degrees. NOWHERE.

Rick choked back the bile rising in his throat. Fear all but paralyzed his body, and only a concentrated force of will caused his right foot to depress the accelerator. He was barely even aware that his passenger, the great Will Arnold, was speaking.

"Hah—this comic's so imaginative. The Ontario story is about a haunted house—just an old shack really, out in the country, not far from Bracebridge. It's been abandoned for years and just left to crumble, but how's this for a spooky kicker? The place doesn't really exist. It's just an image, a mirage. It's nowhere."

A Deal to Die For

"Come on in," a woman's voice called as Bill opened the door. He blinked. The room was huge and extremely, almost painfully, brightly lit. Funny, this casino was his absolute favourite in all of Windsor and he came here pretty regularly, but for some reason he'd never noticed this room before.

Bill looked around, worried that the woman's hollering had disturbed the other gamblers. There was a good crowd of players at the tables, and he didn't want to be disrespectful of their concentration. He was relieved to see that no one seemed to have noticed anything beyond their current personal relationship with the fickle Lady Luck.

"Come on, come on, come on," the woman standing by the corner table repeated. "Close the door. We can't have everyone coming in here—not all at once, anyway."

"Thanks," Bill mumbled. "Maybe this room will change my luck a bit. I sure was having a bad run out there."

"I know, I know. That can happen. You're better off in here, though. So listen, let me tell you how this place works. It's a great find. I've never been happier than since I found this place. I call it my little corner of heaven. It takes a few minutes to get used to it, but let me tell you, after that you're in for a good time."

Bill nodded.

"See, they start you out right here in the corner."

"With you?" Bill asked, still flabbergasted that such a room existed in the gambling spot he thought he knew best.

"Well no, not exactly *with* me. You take over from me," the woman said, taking a step away from the blackjack table to his right.

"Wait," Bill called. "I don't know what to do."

"You'll be fine. You'll catch on. You've got all the time in the world," the woman said before she settled herself at the Texas hold 'em table. Soon she was indistinguishable from any of the other gamblers staring intently at their cards.

Outside the big, bright room, Bill heard a commotion. He pushed the door open and looked toward the black-jack table where he'd spent the afternoon losing money at a furious pace. Something must have happened over there, an accident or something. Paramedics were kneeling down on either side of someone lying on the floor. Everyone looked pretty grim. The medics lifted the person up onto the stretcher. Bill recognized that shirt. It was his shirt. Just before the ambulance attendants covered his body with a sheet, Bill realized that he was dead.

The Dead and Breakfast

I just need to get away for a while, that's all. Nothing's really wrong, of course. This isn't nearly as bad as the last time when I was having those awful spells—not being able to breathe properly and everything. No, it's not a bit like that time. It's only that life seems to have become a little much for me lately. I'm so grateful to Cath for booking me into this B&B. She's been a lifesaver; no one could ask for a better sister, that's for sure.

And look at this place. I mean I've never liked the word "cute," but honestly there's no other way to describe it—it's so cute. I have an entire suite to myself—I didn't expect that. It's lovely. The windows in the living room overlook Lake Ontario. I'm sure I'll spend lots of my time just sitting in that big easy chair over by the window and staring out at the lake.

The bedroom isn't nearly as appealing for some reason, but no matter. Maybe it's just that the bedroom doesn't have the lovely view that the main room does. Oh well, I'm sure it'll be fine.

It's nice to feel hopeful again—even if the hope is only that after my little holiday here I'll feel better, calmer. Obviously I'll still have to take those pills the doctor gave me, but they're absolutely nothing to worry about.

Cath is still over at the main cabin talking to the resort's owner. The drive here didn't take nearly as long as I thought it would, so it's still early. Maybe I'll just lie down and try out the bed while I'm waiting for her to come back. The trip did tire me out, there's no denying it, but I won't let myself fall asleep—at least not until I've said good-bye to Cath. That would be rude and she's been so kind.

You know, now that I look around a bit more, maybe this bedroom isn't going to be so bad after all. I'll just lie down until Cath gets back. The bed's comfortable anyway, except…

I screamed. But no sound came out.

Oh Cath, get here *now*! I can't move and there's someone on the bed with me! Oh dear god. There is. Someone is here. Can't move. Must yell for help. Can't make a sound. Cath, help me! Must've found my voice that time. Oh how they came running—both of them, Cath and the owner. But they were too late. That person who'd been on the bed with me had gone.

What a state all this has left me in. I'll need Cath to stay for a while longer, until I settle down, that's for certain. She will, I know.

I can hear the two of them—the resort owner and my sister—whispering together in the living room. It's hard to make out their exact words over the sound of my heart slamming against my chest. Cath seems to be assuring the owner that everything will be fine. Then she got into her car and drove away just like that. But I'll be all right—as long as that person stays out of my bed. Obviously they'll have to make sure that whoever she is, she keeps to her own room.

Maybe I'll go for a walk along the lake. It's beautiful—so majestic. I have to admit that I'm pleasantly surprised. This area east of Cobourg is much prettier than I thought it would be, especially here along the lake.

The walk was a good idea, but I couldn't stay out very long. I tire so quickly these days. I wish Cath had stayed, if only to see me safely back to my room after this first walk. What if there's a person in my bed again? If there is, I hope that the woman who owns this place believes me.

It'll be all right. I can do this. I can go back into my suite by myself. It'll be easy, just open the door and walk in. Remember the lovely view from the living room? I'll go right to that window, and as I pass the bedroom door I'll just glance in. If the person's still there, I'll just go straight to the main cabin and insist that my room be changed. I don't need anything as big as this suite anyway.

But look, what a relief! There's no one in the bedroom. Everything's fine. Really, sometimes I'm my own worst enemy. It was so silly of me, the whole thing. Imagine me thinking that someone was lying on the bed with me! Of course the whole thing must only have been a figment of my tired old imagination. I could almost laugh at myself for my foolishness. It's just that I so need this little holiday. See, I'm feeling better already. So much better that I'm not worried about lying down for a nap. Perhaps I'll fall asleep…

Oh my, I must have fallen asleep. I can see by the window that it's dark out already. I wonder how long I… That person is in my bed again—lying right next to me—asleep! Oh why can't I move? Wait! She's not asleep. She's dead! Oh dear god. I'm lying beside a dead person.

"You gave us all quite a scare there, Missy," a voice said. "We could hear your carry-on way up the hill at the house. Screaming like a banshee so you were."

It took me a minute to remember who this woman was, but once I did the whole thing came back to me— waking up to find that wretched person in bed with me. I remembered everything right up until the blackness came in. It started at the sides, but it didn't long to spread and rescue me.

"I want Cath," I told the woman. "I want her to take me home."

"Hah, not on your life, Missy. You're staying right here. It's off-season and your Cath, as you call her, is paying me double to keep you here for a week, so believe me, that's exactly what I'm going to do. Now you just toddle off to your rooms and relax. You might as well—you're here for another six days."

My head spun. Paying double? Keeping me here? I know Cath would never be so mean as to abandon me here—or anywhere. I stumbled back to my little cabin. The living room is too sunny, entirely too bright. I need to lie down and close my eyes.

There's an indentation, an outline of a body on the bedspread. I'm sure it's only from when I was lying down before. I'll ease myself down on the bed. Just lay my hands on the bed first.

I screamed again. The mark on the bed was as cold as ice.

I can't tell you what happened next because the blackness came back. When I opened my eyes again I was here, in the hospital. It's awful, so glaringly bright and hideously noisy. I can't turn away because my wrists are bound. My head pounds with pain. Thankfully, I fade away again.

"I've come for my sister's belongings," Cath told the owner of the B&B. "You were supposed to forward them to me."

"I wasn't able to keep my word. I'm sorry. It's been a dreadful couple of weeks here. There was all that carry on with your sister, and earlier last week a guest died—right in the suite you rented for your sister. She seemed perfectly healthy just an hour or so before, then lay down on that bed and died."

The Jacket

Gary pressed down on the accelerator as he cleared the last bend in the S-curve. It was well after midnight and there were no streetlights, but it was a warm summer's night and the sky was clear. Besides, if anyone knew the backroads of northern Ontario, Gary did. In a minute he'd be passing the old burying ground off to the left. That had always been a landmark for him—it meant he was more than halfway home.

A movement in the brush at the side of the road caught his eye and Gary slowed down. He didn't need an animal jumping into the path of his car. He stared toward the bush. Something was definitely making its way toward the road—a deer perhaps?

No! That wasn't a deer. Whatever it was stood upright. Gary's car fishtailed as he slammed on his brakes, but it was too late. A gut-wrenching thud shook the car and he knew he'd hit someone—a girl. He'd seen her clearly in the seconds before the impact. Throwing the shifter into park, he jumped from the car and stood beside it, staring in disbelief.

He'd hit a girl—a girl or a young woman, either way there was no question. He'd hit her and she was dead.

He bent down over the lifeless body, wailing in horror and disbelief at what he had done. "I've gotta do something," he sobbed. "What though? What? What? I can't just leave her here lying dead in the middle of the road."

But nor could he bring himself to lift her into his car. "I've gotta go get help," he told himself, taking off his sports jacket and placing it carefully over the corpse.

He drove to the nearest town, trying to compose himself and to think of the best way to explain what had happened. It sounded insane, but it was true—he'd been driving along a clear patch of roadway when a person had jumped in front of his car and he'd hit her. That was exactly what had happened, so that was what he would say.

It wasn't hard to spot the police station; it was the only building in town with lights glowing in the windows.

There was only one officer on duty, and he took the time to listen carefully to Gary's story.

"You'll be wanting a cup of tea to calm your nerves right about now, I'd imagine," the officer spoke kindly.

"Tea! We don't have time for tea," Gary's voice was strident. "You can't leave that woman's body lying on the road!"

"Have it your way, then," the officer said as he stood up and reached for his keys. "But I think you'll be sorry that you didn't take me up on the offer of a warm drink. Never mind, we'll have it once we're back."

Gary shook with rage. He couldn't believe the disrespect this man was paying—not only to the poor, dead young woman, but also indirectly to every other officer who had ever donned a uniform. This was just no way for a person in authority to behave.

The policeman drove slowly. In the passenger's seat Gary leaned toward the windshield, his palms on the car's dashboard as if trying to push the cruiser to go faster.

"Stop the car!" he cried as they rounded the curve. "Right here. She jumped out in front of my car right here."

The first rays of what would soon become a glorious sunrise shone into the cruiser. The officer turned to Gary. "Before you get out of this car, there's something you need to know. You're not going to find any body out there at the side of the road. You're not going to find anything at all. You're also probably never going to see your sports jacket again."

"You're crazy!" Gary shouted, throwing open the car door and running to the spot where he had left the girl's body. There was no body there.

"See? I was right," the policeman said with pride.

"She was here! I covered her with my jacket and left her here!"

"Son," the policeman said quietly, "what happened to you tonight has been happening on this stretch of road for more than 50 years that I know of—maybe for 50 more before that. Usually the driver who hits her puts her in the back of his car and rushes to the local hospital, except when he gets there the backseat is empty—she's vanished."

"Huh?"

"She's a ghost. You hit a ghost. People know about her; she's a spirit from the old cemetery, that's all. No one talks about it and I'm sure that you won't either, but lots of people have hit her—or they thought they her. The only question this time is what happened to your jacket."

Gary slouched against the hood of the cruiser. "The sun's coming up already. I need to walk this off—starting in that old burial ground."

"Have it your way, son. I'll put the kettle on when I get back to the station. You'll be needing a cup of tea by the time you get there."

Gary waited until the cruiser's taillights disappeared from view before stepping across the culvert and over the dilapidated fence that once neatly surrounded the grave-yard. It was a sad sight. Most of the headstones were old and neglected. Didn't anyone care about any of the people who were buried here? Badly shaken, Gary wandered among the markers until he became overwhelmed. He stood still, closed his eyes and wished blessings to all the departed souls buried there. When he opened his eyes he felt better, strong enough to begin the long walk back to the police station to pick up his car. As he turned to leave he looked down. There, folded neatly beside him, lay his sports jacket. He picked it up. Underneath was a small, flat gravestone: "Sacred to the memory of Sarah Jean, 1832–1855."

"Rest in peace," he told the stone. He put on his jacket and made his way to the road. It was a long walk, but that was all right. He had a lot to think about. The one thing he knew for certain was that he'd take that officer up on his offer of a cup of tea.

The Last Season

Every year when the "boys of summer" hit the Waterloo area, the whole place just came alive. Whenever there was a homestand, the girls and young women all spruced themselves up for the handsome young athletes on the out-of-town teams. Of course as soon as the girls were all gussied up, all the local boys, not just the ones on the baseball team, took notice—no visitors were going to steal *their* girls—so the hometown lads would show the local lasses considerably more attention. It seemed that with baseball season, everyone and everything perked up—even the economy.

Yes sir, baseball just made people happy, and that was a good thing because in the 1930s, there really wasn't much to be happy about. I should know; after all, I was the team's manager for their entire existence. But there's more to the story. It's a sad and puzzling story, actually.

Bert Barrow—he was our star player. That boy had a golden arm, I tell you. How he could pitch. And Bert was no spring chicken, either. He had been a pilot in the Great War. Just the fact that we had our own "flyboy" was enough to do us proud, but then when Bert turned out to be the best pitcher in the league, and a nice guy on top of it all, well, the whole town just came to love him.

Now you might not believe me, but we won the pennant in our starting season—took the playoffs in four straight. At the end of the last inning, everyone was whooping and hollering and celebrating so much that no one noticed Bert wasn't around. Well that guy, he was such a character. Instead of sticking around with the others he ran over to the air strip, and a few minutes later, darned if he didn't fly over the ball diamond, swoop real low and throw a bunch of candies down to the kids. All the while you could hear him yelling "yee haw!" Yup, he was a popular fellow, that Bert.

Later that fall, Bert flew up north to go hunting and never came back. We searched as best we were able, but a ground search wasn't good enough. We needed to hire a pilot and a plane to look for him properly, but we just didn't have that kind of money—things were hard during the Depression. The only person in town who did have the money was the ball club's owner, and he was just too cheap. It was a sad, sad thing, I tell you.

The team took Bert's disappearance hard—well, everyone around did, actually. The next season we didn't even make the playoffs—nor the next, nor the next, nor the next. By then no one was bothering to come out to watch the games, so the owner wasn't making any money. It seemed our hearts had disappeared with Bert.

The winter after that fifth season, the owner sold the club for a pittance. All of us, the players and me, we thought our playing days were over. But this new owner, well, he was an interesting guy. The first thing he did come spring was rent a plane and hire a pilot. It took a more than a week, but finally the pilot spotted the wreckage of Bert's plane. No one knows why, but Bert had crashed into some pretty dense brush.

Well, once we had the coordinates, a bunch of guys went in and found Bert still strapped into the pilot's seat. He had died on impact, it looked like. His poor body had just sat there in that cockpit, rotting, for nearly five years. It was terrible—such disrespect. The only thing we could do was take Bert's body out so we could finally give him a decent burial. People came from all around to attend that funeral and show their respects to Bert.

At the season's home opener a few weeks later, we had a moment of silence. Then we all but blew our opponents out of the ballpark. We won the game by a huge margin, and then the next game and the next and the next until we went on to win the pennant.

It was a glorious moment for all of us, but I think especially for the team's new owner. Some people said it was as if Bert Barrow's once-restless spirit was saying thank you to the man who had finally been responsible for finding his remains. Well, that's what some people said, anyway. Others said Bert's spirit had been so angry about his body being left to rot that he'd put a jinx on that first owner.

I sure do wish that I could tell you the team kept right on winning those baseball seasons, but I can't. Our chances were looking good for the 1939 season, but then the war came and lots of us never played baseball again. Not here on earth anyway. Maybe there were some good innings thrown in the great beyond with Bert on the mound.

There's just one other point I should mention, I guess. The baseball club's first owner, the one who wouldn't do a dead man, his former star pitcher, the courtesy of funding a proper search, well that man lived to be well over 90 years of age, but from the day they found Bert's body, it was as if he was haunted. He never drew another sane breath.

Things in the Closet

We crouched in the very, very back of the closet in the tiny house in Barrie. We made ourselves as small as we possibly could. We barely dared to breathe—from fear of course, but also because of the awful smell.

We could hear it moving around out in the main part of the room. There was absolutely no way of predicting when it would stop the prowling about and settle. Until it did, though, there was nothing we could do but wait. The stress was nearly unbearable. It was almost impossible to stay still, yet our very existence depended on remaining undetected.

Finally the strip of light across the bottom of the door disappeared. It was safe for us. We burst from our hiding spot. It screamed so loud that another one joined it. Just in time we crept back into our hideaway.

"Daniel, you made enough noise to waken the dead. When are you going to get over this? There are no things lurking in your closet."

We receded and once again fought to remain still. We couldn't take any chances. We'd heard tales of things who'd been seen—and those stories *never* ended well at all.

Barbara Smith has always collected folklore, and has successfully combined it with her other passion, writing. A bestselling author of more then 20 books, she has a deep interest in social history and loves historical research so much that she'd rather "research than eat." She has taught creative writing courses at the university and college level and is a charismatic public speaker. Barbara and her husband Bob currently live in Edmonton, Alberta.